THE
REASON
FOR MY
HOPE

THE REASON FOR MY HOPE

CHARLES STANLEY

OLIVER
NELSON

THOMAS NELSON PUBLISHERS
Nashville • Atlanta • London • Vancouver

Published in Nashville, Tennessee, by Thomas Nelson, Inc., Publishers, and distributed in Canada by Word Communications, Ltd., Richmond, British Columbia.

The Bible version used in this publication is THE NEW KING JAMES VERSION. Copyright © 1979, 1980, 1982, Thomas Nelson, Inc., Publishers.

ISBN 0-8407-7765-5 (hardcover)

Printed in the United States of America.
A Crossings Book Club Edition

CONTENTS

Introduction

I Have a Reason to Hope!

If I were to look to the headlines of the newspaper or hear the opening lines of virtually any newscast . . .

If I were to look only at the scores of people I know who struggle daily with severe problems—diseases that have been diagnosed as terminal, marriages that are crumbling, children who are rebellious, communities that are being shattered by racism or eaten away by poverty, homes that are being destroyed by alcohol or chemical addictions . . .

If I were to focus only on the many civil war, intertribal, and religious conflicts that are raging around the world today . . .

If I were to listen only to people who are seeking to escape the horrors of present-day abuse or coping with the fear-evoking memories of past abuse . . .

If I were to keep my mind attuned only to the steady stream of programs on television that are filled with lewdness and violence . . .

It would be easy to lose hope.

But that is not where I look or focus my attention.

I have hope today. It is an unshakable hope. It is a hope based on something eternal and all-powerful. It is a hope founded on good evidence.

The primary reason I'm hopeful today is that I know that I have a personal relationship with God through His Son, Jesus Christ.

My relationship with Jesus Christ gives me an open door to everything that God has promised to His people in His Word. It puts me into direct access to all the resources I will ever need, for any and every circumstance.

I have had enough experiences in my life to know that God is always there when I need Him. He is *reliably* there. He is *certain* to be there at all times. I have absolute assurance that no matter what happens in my life, He is in control of my life—perfectly present, able, and at work—and since He is absolutely and completely sovereign, nothing can happen to me that is apart from His ultimate will for my life.

Because I know that God loves me perfectly and knows me intimately, I have hope in every situation. No matter what happens to me, I can't lose!

Even in what have appeared to be the worst possible circumstances in my personal life, I have been, and continue to be, hopeful. I may appear to be suffering loss on the outside, but I am winning on the inside. Why? Because I am always looking to the Lord. He is a victorious Lord; failure and futility are totally alien to His nature. He imparts to me His victory, His righteousness, His perspective, His wisdom, His faith.

That does not mean that I am in denial about bad circumstances. I live in the real world and have real problems just like everybody else. But I refuse to be defeated by bad circumstances. They do not have a hold on me. They don't fill me with fear or cause me to live in dread. Certainly, many days are filled with problems that are so large, if I looked only at them and at nothing else, I could easily give way to despair. But if I'm always looking to God from the midst of my circumstances, then I always have reason to hope. He is above, beyond, and greater than my problems. He is active in my problems. And He is at work resolving my problems for my ultimate good and eternal future.

With that perspective, how can I not be hopeful? I am linked to the sovereign and almighty King of the universe. He is my heavenly Father. He controls my life and desires a highly favorable outcome for me.

He is the anchor that always holds, no matter how severe the storm may be.

And He gives us very specific reasons on which each of us can base hope. If you are without hope today, or if you have a loved one who is without hope, these are reasons you need to know about and take into your life. This book is for you!

> *My hope is built on nothing less*
> *Than Jesus' blood and righteousness;*
> *I dare not trust the sweetest frame,*
> *But wholly lean on Jesus' name.*
> *On Christ, the solid rock, I stand;*
> *All other ground is sinking sand,*
> *All other ground is sinking sand.*
>
> *When darkness veils his lovely face,*
> *I rest on his unchanging grace;*
> *In every high and stormy gale,*
> *My anchor holds within the veil.*
> *On Christ, the solid rock, I stand;*
> *All other ground is sinking sand,*
> *All other ground is sinking sand.*
>
> *His oath, his covenant, his blood*
> *Support me in the whelming flood;*
> *When all around my soul gives way,*
> *He then is all my hope and stay.*
> *On Christ, the solid rock, I stand;*
> *All other ground is sinking sand,*
> *All other ground is sinking sand.*

When he shall come with trumpet sound,
O may I then in him be found!
Dressed in his righteousness alone,
Faultless to stand before the throne.
On Christ, the solid rock, I stand;
All other ground is sinking sand,
All other ground is sinking sand.

—Edward Mote, 1797–1874
"The Solid Rock"

CHAPTER 1

CREATED TO BE LOVERS

Have you ever wondered about your purpose in life? Have you ever wondered why God created you and what He has destined for you? Have you ever asked yourself, What is my reason for getting up in the morning?

At the core of the depression and despair that many people feel is a nagging question: Why am I here? The fact is, if you don't know why you are here, then you don't have a sense of purpose, direction, or meaning in your life. If you are without a basic mooring for your soul, spirit, and mind, then it is very easy to lose hope. If you don't know why you are alive right now, then it is very difficult to see any reason for why you may continue to be alive in the future. The very nature of hope requires that you have some sense of meaning and purpose for your life.

The Word of God says that you have a purpose, one that is both noble and highly desirable in the mind and heart of virtually every person who has ever lived: *You were created by God to love and be loved.*

Yes, you.

This statement is certainly true for all of humankind, but it is also a truth that is meant for you to embrace personally. God loves *you*. He loves you unconditionally, without limit or qualification, and He loves you personally and individually.

Not only does He love you and desire to shower you with His love, but He longs to be loved by you.

Furthermore, He desires that you love and be loved by other human beings. God is generous—even extravagant—in His love. He delights when you express His brand of unconditional love to others and when you experience that kind of love in return.

If I could use only one word to describe God's nature and His desire for you, it would be *love*.

The Unfathomable Depth of God's Love

The very essence of God's being—His personality, His nature—is love. The motivation for God's sending Jesus into the world was love. The most famous verse in all the Bible tells us this: "God so loved the world that He gave His only begotten Son" (John 3:16 NKJV).

The reason that Jesus came to this earth, lived a victorious life, and then died as the one definitive and lasting sacrifice to reunite God and human beings was love. God desires to have a relationship with you. He desires to reveal Himself to you, to shower His love and good gifts upon you, and to live with you forever.

The apostle John told us in one of his letters that the supreme attribute of God is love. John based that conclusion on his personal relationship with Jesus, having walked with Him for nearly three years of ministry before Jesus' crucifixion and resurrection. He wrote this after having lived in relationship with the Lord Jesus for several decades after Jesus went to be with the Father:

We have seen and testify that the Father has sent the Son as Savior of the world. Whoever confesses that Jesus is the Son of God, God abides in him, and he in God. And we have known and believed the love that God has for us. God is love, and he who abides in love abides in God, and God in him. (1 John 4:14–16 NKJV)

Note this one little phrase in the passage: "known and believed the love that God has for us." John *believed* that God loved him.

John tended to refer to himself in his writings not by his name but as "the one whom Jesus loved." That was especially true in the gospel of John. He certainly didn't mean that Jesus loved him in an exclusive way. John did not say that with pride; rather, he had great humility, in essence conveying that he, of all people, knew the love of God. John was acknowledging that he was nobody without the love of Christ. It was the hallmark of his identity, even more than his own name. Christ's love meant everything to him.

Remember that John was called one of the "Sons of Thunder" in the Gospels. He no doubt was a sometimes boisterous, always passionate, periodically rambunctious, perhaps even an impetuous man—a fisherman who was truly a man's man in every sense. John's world was a world that was ruled by Rome, determined to a great extent by the forces of nature and the catch of the day, and spiritually dictated by the gloom-and-doom Pharisees and Sadducees who emphasized obedience to the law of God but had little to say about the love of God. John was bold enough to grab hold of his destiny with both hands and not let go. He was brave enough to follow Jesus and to trust Him explicitly.

Have you ever thought about what it took to be a disciple in the time of Jesus? To give up everything and follow Him on a daily basis, not knowing where you were going to spend the night, what you were going to eat, or what forces of evil you might encounter? The apostles were men of courage.

They were also men who knew what it meant to be loved thoroughly. There is little reason to give up everything you have acquired or have known as your identity and to follow another person unless you are compelled by that person's vision for the future and by the depth of that person's love for you. Following a vision for the future is not enough; such a vision eventually will pale or may even be seen as manipulative or evil unless that vision for the future is rooted in a highly personal and deep love relationship. John and the other disciples knew that kind of love from Jesus. As John said, "We have known . . . the love that God has for us." John's belief was based upon experience—not only while Jesus was alive, but his experience by faith in the years after Jesus' return to heaven.

John believed he was a beloved one of Christ. He embraced that love wholeheartedly. He staked his life on the fact that God loved him.

The sad reality is that many people today have heard that God loves them, but they simply don't *believe* it. They don't know the full reality of God's love in their lives. They haven't experienced it, and therefore, they don't know how to embrace it, nurture it, or grow in it.

Experiencing God's Love in Your Life

A man once confessed to me, "I hear people talk about love, but I don't know what love is. Oh, I can comprehend with my mind what they are saying. I can understand the words they use to describe how they feel. But I don't know what love feels like."

I knew exactly how that man felt. I once felt the same way. Most of my life I had an ache to feel loved.

I didn't know a lot about love as a child. My father died of kidney disease when I was only nine months old. My mother immediately went to work to support us the best she could. For the first couple of years of my life, various women took care of me while my mother worked, but once I started school, I was pretty much on my own. At the age of five, I learned to comb my own hair, dress myself, cook my own breakfast, and get myself to school. My mother didn't get back each day until well after I returned home from school.

Even during the brief periods through the years when we lived with my aunts and uncles, I suffered from loneliness. I knew my mother cared for me, but I didn't feel an abiding sense of love. On more occasions than I can begin to count, the comforting arms, tender touches, and words of love that I needed as a child were missing. Nobody was present to provide them when I needed them.

When I was nine years old, my mother married a man who was full of anger, hostility, and bitterness. My stepfather was mean and abusive. I never heard him say a positive word about anything, much less a word of care or love. I don't recall his ever giving me anything, including a compliment, a word of praise, or even an expression of concern.

During my twelfth year, I went to church one morning and went forward when Mrs. Wilson, who was preaching a revival at our church, gave the altar call. I fell on my knees, and I cried and prayed and asked the Lord to save me. I told Him that I believed in Jesus and His death and resurrection. When the pastor asked me to come up and tell the people what the Lord had done for me, I remember standing behind that pulpit and saying, "I don't know everything He's done for me, but I know He's saved me." I had absolutely no doubt that I had been forgiven and that I was destined for eternal life.

Knowing that I was saved, however, did not mean that I had felt the love of God in my heart. My basic concept of God was one of judgment, not love. In my view, He was a remote, hard, and harsh God. Oh, I may have been able to quote a Bible verse about God's love, and if someone had point-blank asked me, "Does God love you?" I would have said yes. But that was information I had learned in my mind; it wasn't something that I felt in my heart.

Much of my concept of God was formed, of course, by my early childhood experiences. That is true for every person. My mother was a Christian, but she didn't talk much about God around me. When we prayed, we both used King James English. For years, I thought that praying with "Thees" and "Thous" was the only way a person could be heard in heaven! Both in language and in daily living, God seemed very distant.

Because God wasn't very near, He wasn't very accessible or dependable. I couldn't count on Him being present when I needed Him. I never thought about Him as being God the *Father*. Father—which in my case was stepfather—was a concept that was too earthly, too human, too familiar and, in many ways, too painful. God was, to me, remote and yet always watching and listening—ready to put me down and drive me out if I erred too badly.

My mother's constant admonition to me as a boy was, "Don't do anything that you wouldn't want to be caught doing if Jesus were to come." That really put a crimp in my style since just about everything that a normal boy would consider to be fun, my mother and the church considered to be a sin. In those days, reading the funny paper was a sin. Wearing a tie clasp was a sin. Listening to any kind of music other than hymns was a sin. The God who saved me that Sunday morning was the same God who created the Ten Commandments, who kept points and checked your life's scoreboard periodically, and who could and would send you to hell for your unrepented sins. I was saved, spared, but that had very little to do with love.

God Loves Us Unconditionally

From God's standpoint, salvation has everything to do with love. Love was the motivation for His creating us, sustaining us, and sending His Son to die for our sins. But as a twelve-year-old, I didn't know that.

And the equal fact is that I don't need to feel God's love to be saved. Salvation is based on answering one question and one question alone: Am I willing by faith to receive Jesus Christ as my personal Savior based on the fact that when Jesus died on Calvary, He paid my sin debt in full? If I say yes to that question, I receive Christ into my life. When I receive Him, I receive Him by faith. I believe in Him as my personal Savior. I accept a free gift offered to me with open arms. I don't need to know anything about the motivation for God to extend that gift to me. I only need to receive it.

Repentance—which is our response to sin after we have accepted God's forgiveness—is something that we do by the will. We choose to turn away from sin because something has happened in our hearts. We choose to walk in a way that is pleasing to God. Again, our motivation for repentance does not rely upon feelings of love. We can repent solely out of obedience and a desire to do what is right in God's sight. We don't need to feel a great outpouring of love for God, or feel His great outpouring of love for us, to convince us to obey His commandments and lead a godly life. Some do, of course. But many people don't feel anything related to love in accepting Jesus as their Savior and making a decision to follow Him as their Lord.

On the one hand, of course, this is highly desirable. Our salvation is not dependent upon our emotions, which can be very capricious and unstable. Salvation is rooted in our acceptance of what Christ did, not in the way we feel.

On the other hand, when we accept Christ and don't have a good concept of God's love, we can continue to live a long time with a sense of fear, dread, and suspicion related to God. We can continue to strive to be worthy of our salvation and to do our utmost to "be good enough" for God's rewards. I know that to be true; I did just that for decades.

I was an ambitious teenager, working hard to escape my impoverished childhood. When the opportunity arose for me to go to college, I threw myself into my studies. When I became a pastor, I threw myself 110 percent into doing everything I could for my congregation. I didn't just try hard—I drove myself. I made serious lists of lofty goals and then threw myself into achieving them, even before my schedule called for their accomplishment and to a degree that was beyond the goals I had set! I had absolutely no tolerance for laziness or slothfulness, in myself or anybody else. I had a perfectionist's attitude—do all you can do and then do a bit more.

My life was ruled by shoulds and oughts: "I should do this; I ought to do that." I didn't want God's approval alone. I also wanted the approval of those who called me their pastor or colleague in ministry.

If a person has never known genuine *unconditional* love, then he knows the rules only for *conditional* love. And the foremost rule for conditional love is: "You must earn the right to be loved." In my case, I felt I needed to earn the right to be loved by others, and I needed to earn the privilege of having been saved by an all-powerful, all-knowing, judgmental God. If I had any hope of receiving eternal rewards from God, I needed to earn them by my effort in ways that were measurable or definable.

The end result of that approach to life is one of constant striving and constant irritation or frustration.

No matter how much you push yourself, you never feel as if you are doing enough.

No matter how much you push others to be perfect, they never are.

The more you attempt to control, the less control you feel you have. The more you are critical, the more you find to criticize. The more you engage in fighting "for what is best," the more you lose the relationships that hold the greatest potential for giving you the one thing you need—love.

I wanted God's approval. I never even dreamed it might be possible to have God's love.

That may sound strange to you coming from a pastor. The sad fact is that I used to be a preacher who said very little about God's unconditional love. I didn't have anything to say! I once asked my secretary to do a search of the files and pull for me any sermon I had ever preached on God's love. She pulled one sermon—out of decades' worth of hundreds of sermons—and when I read it, it wasn't worth the paper it was typed on. I didn't know anything at the heart level about God's love. I therefore couldn't preach anything *from* the heart about it. I knew about God's love only at the head level.

What happens to a person who knows about God's love only at the mind or intellectual level? Such a person has a theory, but not an experience. A love void continues to exist, and over time, that void grows larger and becomes more frustrating. I believe that is especially true if a person is continuing to seek God and to desire all that God has for him or her.

Now, I didn't know that I was missing the love of God in my life. All I knew was that *something* was missing in my Christian experience. I would preach about the freedom that Christ gives, go home, look up to heaven, and say, "But what about me? Why don't I feel free?" I had an ache within me that I could not define or eliminate and, eventually, could not escape.

My Personal Encounter with God's Great Love

In intense inner pain and turmoil, I sought advice from four men whom I trusted explicitly. I called the men, who are people of the highest integrity, and I asked them to meet with me to hear me out with empathy and then to give me their wise counsel. I trusted God to help them to help me.

I met with the four men privately at a lodge in a wilderness area. I confessed to them that I was at the end of myself. I didn't know what to do. I didn't know where to go. I asked them if I could share with them my life and told them that after they had heard my story, I wanted them to give me their best advice. I assured them that I would do whatever they advised me to do. I had that much respect for them. I also conveyed to them how desperate I was and how extremely serious I was about receiving their help. They generously agreed to hear me out and to be God's instruments in my life.

I talked all afternoon and evening. I woke up several times in the middle of the night and wrote a total of seventeen pages in longhand—legal-sized pages—of things I wanted to be sure to tell them the next morning. I told them everything I remembered about my early life and all the highlights—both painful and positive—of my adult life and ministry. When I was finished—and believe me, I was completely spent at that point—I said, "Now, whatever you tell me to do, I'll do it."

They asked me two or three questions, and then one of the men who was sitting directly across the table from me said, "Charles, put your head on the table and close your eyes." I did. He said to me very kindly, "Charles, I want you to envision your father picking you up in his arms and holding you." After a few moments, he said, "What do you feel?"

I burst out crying. And I cried and I cried and I cried. I could not stop crying. Finally, when I stopped, he asked me again, "What do you feel?" I said, "I feel warm, loved, secure. I feel good." And I started weeping again.

For the first time in my life, I felt emotionally that God loved me. I had known as a fact from His Word that God loved me. I had believed by faith that God loved me. I had accepted the fact that love is God's nature. But until that day, not very many years ago, I had never emotionally felt God loving me.

God used that encounter with those four men, and that one simple question, to unlock the love void in my life and to begin to pour into it a flood of His divine love.

The full release of God's love didn't happen in a day. It was a process, little by little. But the more I explored the love of God, the more God began to reveal my true identity in Christ—that I belonged to Him as I had never belonged to anybody, that I was worth something to Him, and that He loved me beyond measure. I discovered when I got to the end of myself and all of my efforts at striving for perfection, a kind and gracious heavenly Father who had been loving me unconditionally all my life. Let me assure you, nothing is more liberating than that discovery.

The more I experienced God's love, the more I began to understand the importance of saying to others, "God loves you just the way you are." I came to be able to love others as they were and to be far less critical of their failed efforts or lack of perfection. God's love for me became the source of a great love for others. The outpouring of God's love into my life positively affected my ministry and my relationships with others. I had been invaded by love, and I couldn't keep it to myself.

From that day in the mountains, I had a sense of inner closeness with God that I had never experienced before. I knew I could trust Him regardless of what happened to me, regardless of any mistakes I might make, regardless of how I might respond or react in my humanity. I had a strong feeling of assurance that I had always been loved, was loved now, and would always be loved with a vast love that was beyond my comprehension, but that I could experience nonetheless on a daily basis.

Once intimacy with God has been established, it grows. There is no end to God's love, and there ultimately will be no end to our ability to experience it. We need never have love-starved hearts again. His desire is to overflow us with His love and, all the while, to enlarge our capacity to experience His love and give it to others.

I came to the place where I could say with the apostle John, "I have known the love of God. I *believe* the love of God." I stand in that place today. The great desire of my heart is that you might know and believe that God loves you.

The Nature of God's Great Love

Let me assure you of several things related to God's love.

First, God's love is the most important thing you can know about God.

In Luke 10:25–28 (NKJV) we read about an encounter that Jesus had with a certain religious expert. This lawyer (who knew the Law of Moses extremely well) asked Jesus, as if testing Him, "Teacher, what shall I do to inherit eternal life?" Jesus asked him in return, "What is written in the law? What is your reading of it?" The man answered, "'You shall love the LORD your God with all your heart, with all your soul, with all your strength, and with all your mind,' and 'your neighbor as yourself.'" The religious expert was quoting from two passages in the Law of Moses: Deuteronomy 6:5 and Leviticus 19:18. Jesus replied, "You have answered rightly; do this and you will live."

The most important decision you can ever make in your life is a decision about love—to receive God's love, to love God, and to love others.

There are some 185 references to God's love in the Bible, 140 of them in the New Testament. In Greek, the language in which the New Testament was written originally, the word that refers to God's love is *agape*. This is sacrificial, divine love. God extends this type of love to each of us, and He desires for us to show it to others.

God's love is absolute. It does not waver. It does not change over time. It cannot be influenced by circumstances or situations. It cannot be diminished.

Whatever we might say about God Himself, we must say about God's love. His love is powerful. It penetrates and causes change in the human heart. It has purpose. It holds infinite meaning in its every expression.

God's love is never subject to favoritism. He loves the sinner as much as He loves the saint. That may be a fact that we find hard to swallow in our human pride, or our desire to be "somebody special," but the fact remains. God loves each of His children with the same quantity and quality of love. The difference between sinner and saint is that the person who has accepted God's forgiveness and God's love is in a position to receive all of the blessings that accompany His outpouring of love into her life. The person who has turned away from God has put himself out of a position to know the fullness of God's blessings. It is as if a mighty river of God's love is flowing toward him, but he has built for himself an island in the middle of the river so that none of the love touches his being.

Let me carry that illustration one degree further. A person who has alienated himself from God might plant bushes and trees on his island in the midst of God's river. The plants might flourish, and he might enjoy the fruit they produce. The plants, of course, are drawing from the river through their roots. The end result is that the person experiences God-given things related to God's love. This is certainly true for every person. The Bible tells us that the rain falls on the just and the unjust, the sun shines on the saint and the sinner. Every person experiences certain benefits and blessings that are the gifts of a loving God, regardless of whether he believes that God exists.

The person living on an island in the midst of God's river of love may even dip periodically into that river to take a drink. Many people who don't know God still have periodic feelings of love— perhaps as a feeling they have in their relationship with another person, a sensation that is triggered by deeply inspiring music or an awesome sunset, or an emotion that occurs when they are carried away by the beauty or mystery of something. But these experiences tend to be isolated in time and space. They are events, not an ever-present experience of love.

A person can live and die on his island—and know a certain degree of love—without ever setting foot into the river or allowing himself to be washed by its cleansing, freeing, invigorating, exhilarating currents.

God's love is flowing toward each one of us as a deep, wide, beautiful, and never-ending river. It is up to us to jump in.

God's love is also unconditional. It is not based upon what we do, what we have, or what we achieve. His love is given to us because of who we are, His creation. It is not grounded on any other premise or motivation.

You can't earn unconditional love. You can't merit it in any way. You can't deserve it. God says you are worthy of His love solely because it is His desire to love you. There is nothing you can do to win more of God's love. In fact, *you can't get God to love you any more than He already does.*

Because God's love is unconditional and not based upon your performance, accept it, receive it, and delight in it.

Second, the most important response you can make to God's love is to love Him in return.

John said it simply and eloquently, "We love Him because He first loved us" (1 John 4:19 NKJV).

Jesus said that the first and foremost commandment was this: "You shall love the LORD your God with all your heart, with all your soul, and with all your mind" (Matt. 22:37 NKJV). The only response acceptable to God's great outpouring of love toward you is to love Him back.

You can choose not to do so. You can rebel against God's love and turn your back on God's outstretched arms. You can even deny the existence of God's love. That doesn't change God's love toward you, but it does do something in you.

The person who stubbornly refuses to acknowledge and receive God's love cuts herself off from great blessing. Not only that, but such a person quickly yields to anger, hatred, resentment, and bitterness. To harden one's heart against God's love is the supreme act of rebellion. The person who does this is hurting herself the most.

Loving God is a commandment in God's Word because like following all the commandments, loving God brings good into our lives. It is not a commandment because God fears that we will not love Him unless He commands us to do so. Rather, it is a commandment because God alone is worthy to be loved. It is the only appropriate response to make toward One who loves as He loves. There is no other acceptable or honorable response we can make. It's as if we are being told, "There's only one right thing to do, so do it."

In spite of what you may have been told in your life, in spite of what you may have come to believe, there is no reason *not* to love God. Some people don't because they have bought into a lie from Satan about the nature of God. They don't love God because they have been convinced by the enemy of their souls that to love and obey God is to be less of a person. They have bought into Satan's lie that God causes bad things to happen to good people—as if God is enjoying some kind of joke on the human race. I have met countless people who are mad at God because of something they think God did to them unfairly and without cause.

Friend, that is never the case. God doesn't hurt people because it gives Him pleasure. He doesn't abuse His creation. Jesus said, "The thief [the devil] does not come except to steal, and to kill, and to destroy. I have come that they may have life, and that they may have it more abundantly" (John 10:10 NKJV).

The devil always plays to our pride. He constantly attempts to convince us that if we love God, we will have less personal freedom, less personal identity, and less pleasure. The end of that lie, however, is always tragic. Those who rebel against God's love inevitably find their freedom is dashed. If they don't wind up in a literal prison, they wind up in an emotional or psychological prison. They may wind up in a prison called addiction or in a prison of hatred and anger. Those who rebel against God's love inevitably find that they lose their identity; they gain a reputation that totally denies their goodness and dignity. Those who rebel against God's love also find that they end up with no pleasure in life. They become jaded, cynical, critical and, in the end, apathetic to virtually everything. They have the ultimate "been there, done that" attitude.

On the other hand, those who embrace God's love and return it enjoy an inner freedom they never imagined. They find that they are more themselves and that they have hidden talents, abilities, and capacities they never knew. The joy of perpetual discovery is theirs. They know true delight in God's creation.

All of the reasons *not* to love God are of human origin and, to a great extent, contrived. They are not rooted in any lasting reality. The *only* satisfying, enriching, meaningful, and joyous response to God's love is to love Him in return!

"But why is loving God a commandment?" you may ask.

The purpose of God's commandments ultimately is not to keep you from doing things that you find pleasurable or fun, but to guide you toward doing things that will bring you the greatest possible good in life.

In Deuteronomy 6, where you first find the great commandment to love God with the heart, soul, and strength, you also find this commandment: "You shall fear the LORD your God and serve Him" (v. 13 NKJV). Fear in this regard is not dreadful fright but an "awesome awe." You are to recognize how mighty and glorious God is, that He is holy and almighty, and out of your overwhelming awe that such a God can and does love you personally, you are to obey Him as your supreme King.

And another commandment in the same chapter is this:

> *You shall not tempt the LORD your God. . . . You shall diligently keep the commandments of the LORD your God, His testimonies, and His statutes which He has commanded you. And you shall do what is right and good in the sight of the LORD, that it may be well with you, and that you may go in and possess the good land of which the LORD swore to your fathers, to cast out all your enemies from before you, as the LORD has spoken.* (vv. 16–19 NKJV)

Note the specific blessings that come when you do what the Lord has commanded in His Word:

That it may be well with you. There is a personal blessing to be enjoyed—a peace of mind, a wholeness of being, a sense of purpose and meaning in life. "That it may be well with you" includes having hope!

Possess the good land. Someone who obeys God explicitly and diligently is in a position to receive material blessing from God.

Cast out all your enemies. God's blessing extends to your relationships. You will not have to do battle with other people. Your relationships will be in good order; friendships, marriage, and parent-child relationships will be subject to God's design. And when they are, you will enjoy a great exchange of love with other people.

What a marvelous promise of God to someone who loves Him! What more could you desire than to have things go well in life, to be blessed materially, and to have wonderful relationships with other people?

You shall teach the commandments of God to your children. This theme runs throughout Deuteronomy 6. God's people are commanded to teach God's statutes to their children and to bind them to their lives and to their homes. God's people are to convey the understanding that "the LORD commanded us to observe all these statutes, to fear the LORD our God, for our good always" (Deut. 6:24 NKJV).

So many people I have met seem to believe that God's commandments are intended to stifle human beings—to deny us pleasure, to keep us from experiencing the "good life." The exact opposite is true. God's commandments are for our good *always*. God made us, and He knows our limitations, our drives, our weaknesses. He also knows what will give us the greatest sense of fulfillment, satisfaction, meaning, purpose, and hope. He knows what will put us into the best possible position to give and receive love from other people. His commandments are His operating instructions so that we might experience all of the wonderful things that He desires to give us. His commandments have been given so that we might be part of a "holy people . . . a people for Himself, a special treasure" (Deut. 7:6 NKJV).

Furthermore, God is "the faithful God who keeps covenant and mercy for a thousand generations with those who love Him and keep His commandments" (Deut. 7:9 NKJV). God's covenant is something you can always count on holding firm.

The very essence of God's covenant with His people is intended to be love. He loves us. He desires only that we love Him in return. If we love Him, we will obey Him—without question, without hesitation, without holding anything back. Our obedience will be spontaneous and wholehearted. And such obedience carries with it reward. The obedient are not swayed by temptations. They are not easy prey for those with evil intent. In sidestepping evil, they experience God's goodness. This goodness is detailed in Deuteronomy 7:13–15 (NKJV):

> *He will love you and bless you and multiply you; He will also bless the fruit of your womb and the fruit of your land, your grain and your new wine and your oil, the increase of your cattle and the offspring of your flock, in the land of which He swore to your fathers to give you. You shall be blessed above all peoples. . . . And the LORD will take away from you all sickness, and will afflict you with none of the terrible diseases of Egypt which you have known.*

Loving God is a commandment that carries with it an abundant blessing. Indeed, you can never outlove God. The more you love Him, the more you will be able to experience His love. He enlarges your capacity to know Him and receive from Him, but His outpouring of love is always at the overflow level in spite of how much you grow.

Third, God's love is your ultimate reason to have hope.

If you know with certainty that God loves you and that He desires good for you, what is there to fear? What is there to dread? What is there to be depressed about?

I am not making light of fears, doubts, or depression. They are normal human responses. Hope, however, compels you not to remain in a state of fear, doubt, or depression. Hope encourages you to raise your eyes and look for the dawning of a new day. Hope calls you to anticipate God's best.

Make this your number one reason for hope today:

_____

I have hope because I know God loves me.

_____

CHAPTER 2

GOD HAS A MASTER PLAN

A young woman once came to me, with tears streaming down her cheeks, and said, "Pastor, everything in my life is confused. I don't know whom to believe, what I can count on, or whom I can trust. The ground underneath my feet seems to be shifting at all times. Nothing seems clear or certain."

She began to tell me her story. Her husband had left her, but he couldn't really give her a good reason for why he had left. She suspected that there might be another woman in his life, but he denied that. She asked him repeatedly why he had abandoned their marriage, but he gave different and vague answers each time. Various family members and friends gave her their opinions and bits of advice, none of which truly satisfied the ache in her heart or answered the questions that filled her mind. Some of the information given to her was contradictory. Everybody seemed to have his or her own agenda for the situation, and nobody seemed to have any sure answers or reliable facts.

Her life was in chaos.

And her responses to chaos were natural—she was confused and also afraid. Her body language spoke loudly about fear. She sat with her arms folded tightly around her body, her legs were crossed, and she sat hunched over. After listening to her pour out her heart for about twenty minutes, I asked her, "Are you afraid?"

With the tears flowing freely once again, she said, "Yes, I am. I don't know what's going to happen."

I said, "Let's start at that point because it really is the most critical." And then I paused a moment. "Let me ask you a question: Whom do you believe?"

She said, "I don't know. I don't know if I can believe anybody."

I said, "What about God?"

She said very matter-of-factly, "Oh, I believe in God."

I said, "Yes, but do you *believe* God."

"What do you mean?" she asked.

"Believing in God and believing God are two different things. Believing in God is saying in your heart, 'I know God exists.' Jesus said that even the demons believe *in* God. But believing God is believing everything God has said about Himself, about us, and about the relationship He desires to have with us."

She thought about that for a few moments, and then she said thoughtfully and sincerely, "I never thought about it that way. I know I'm a Christian. I've accepted Jesus into my heart and I know I'm saved. Is that what you mean?"

I said, "That's a big part of believing God—to believe that God sent Jesus to be our Savior, to believe that God has made a way for us to be forgiven of our sinful nature, to believe that He loved us so much that He sent His only begotten Son so that we might accept Him and have eternal life."

She laughed a little nervously and said, "But there's more, right?"

"Right," I said. "There's far more that God has said to us in His Word about the relationship He desires to have with us *after* we are saved. Let me share a few verses of Scripture with you."

I opened my Bible to this passage and let her read it:

Do not fear those who kill the body but cannot kill the soul. But rather fear Him who is able to destroy both soul and body in hell. Are not two sparrows sold for a copper coin? And not one of them falls to the ground apart from your Father's will.

But the very hairs of your head are all numbered. Do not fear therefore; you are of more value than many sparrows. (Matt. 10:28–31 NKJV)

I asked her, "Do you believe that God doesn't want you to be afraid today?"

"Yes," she said, "based upon what this says, I do believe that God doesn't want me to be afraid."

I asked, "Do you believe that God knows all about you—even the number of hairs on your head?"

"Yes," she said, "I believe that."

"And do you believe that God knows what is happening to you?"

"Yes."

"Do you believe that you are valuable to God?"

She hesitated for a moment and then said, "Yes."

I turned to Jesus' words in Matthew 28:20 (NKJV): "Lo, I am with you always, even to the end of the age."

I asked her, "Do you believe that Jesus is with you right now, and that He will continue to be with you every moment of every day for the rest of your life?"

"Yes," she said, "I believe that."

I turned quickly to 2 Timothy 1:7 (NKJV): "For God has not given us a spirit of fear, but of power and of love and of a sound mind."

She anticipated my question and said with a genuine smile, "Yes, Pastor, I believe that God has not given me a spirit of fear, but of power and of love and of a sound mind."

"You truly believe that He is going to give you the strength and the love and the wisdom to face this confusion in your life?"

"Yes," she said. "I believe God."

Next, I turned to James 1:2–5 (NKJV), which says,

My brethren, count it all joy when you fall into various trials, knowing that the testing of your faith produces patience. But let patience have its perfect work, that you may be perfect and complete, lacking nothing. If any of you lacks wisdom, let him ask of God, who gives to all liberally and without reproach, and it will be given to him.

I said, "If you don't know what to do, the only thing to do is to wait and see what God will do and what God will reveal to you. That's what having patience means. It doesn't mean to sit and do nothing, but to wait and watch, always looking to God to see what He will do. Do you believe that God's desire for you in this situation is for you to have patience and to trust Him?"

"Yes," she said, "I believe that."

"And do you believe that if you ask God for wisdom anytime you have doubts, fears, or questions, He will reveal His wisdom to you?"

"Yes," she said.

Finally, I turned to Romans 8:28 (NKJV): "We know that all things work together for good to those who love God, to those who are the called according to His purpose."

I said to her, "You have told me that you love God and that you have accepted Jesus as your Savior. That means you are called according to His purpose. Do you believe that all things are going to work together for your good—that God isn't going to let anything come out of this ultimately that will destroy you or be for evil in your life?"

She thought for a few minutes, and tears began to form again in her eyes. Then she looked me straight in the eye and said, "Yes, Pastor, I believe that."

"You believe God is going to be true to His Word?"

"Yes," she said. "I believe God."

She left my pastor's study that day with a different countenance. She had a smile on her face, a boldness to her step, and a confidence in the way she held her head.

What made the difference?

She chose to believe God—to believe that His Word was not only truth, but also true for her and for her situation.

When life's circumstances and troubles throw us into panic and confusion, all of life feels chaotic. We start asking, "What's going on? Has God lost control?"

Chaos produces fear in us. No one likes the feeling of things being out of control. The natural response is to be afraid and to have doubts. When those times come, we must remind ourselves of one supreme fact: *God has a plan and He is in control.*

God Never Loses Control

The disciples of Jesus knew what it meant to experience chaos and to have doubt and fear. One evening Jesus said to them, "Let us cross over to the other side."

Jesus had a plan!

The disciples got into a boat with Jesus, and as they made their way to the other side of the Sea of Galilee, a tremendous storm arose. The Bible says, "The waves beat into the boat, so that it was already filling." Jesus, meanwhile, was asleep on a pillow in the stern of the boat. The disciples awoke Jesus and said to Him, "Do You not care that we are perishing?" They had doubt. They felt fear. Their universe was in chaos in that storm, and they had no other thought than for the safety of their lives.

Jesus arose and rebuked the wind, saying to the sea, "Peace, be still!" The wind ceased, and there was a great calm. Jesus asked His disciples, "Why are you so fearful? How is it that you have no faith?" The disciples had no answer. Perhaps they were speechless in their amazement. With a single sentence, Jesus had brought peace to their chaos.

And the very next verse says, "Then they came to the other side of the sea." (See Mark 4:35–5:1 NKJV.)

The disciples and Jesus arrived just as Jesus said they would. He had a plan, and it was fulfilled.

God works the very same way in our lives today. He calls us to have faith in Him and to believe that He is in charge—that He has a plan and that His plan will be fulfilled. He asks us to use our faith to speak peace to the storms in our lives. He gives us His Word as our confidence, our assurance, that He is in control.

When we are in chaos, we lose sight of hope; we feel we are on the brink of perishing.

When we remind ourselves that God has a plan, and that He is bringing His plan to full fruition, then we grow in hope. We have an increased expectancy that God is in control, and in that lies peace for our hearts and minds.

Just before His arrest and crucifixion, Jesus asked His disciples, "Do you now believe? Indeed the hour is coming, yes, has now come, that you will be scattered, each to his own, and will leave Me alone. And yet I am not alone, because the Father is with Me. These things I have spoken to you, that in Me you may have peace" (John 16:31–33 NKJV).

Jesus had the peace of the Father with Him. He knew that God was in control of all that would happen. And Jesus wanted His disciples to know the same peace and to have the same confidence that God was at work, revealing and executing His plan for the ages.

Do you believe God today? Do you believe He is in control of His plan?

God Has a Plan for All Creation

Have you ever stared in wonder through a telescope? How about a microscope?

You no doubt were amazed at the vastness of God's creation. Our finite minds cannot fathom the extremes of the universe in which we are so carefully positioned. We stand in awe of the beauty and intricacy of God's designs.

Those who truly study God's creation surely must stand in awe of the myriad of interlocking laws, principles, and systems built into creation. God's creation is not haphazard or in chaos. It operates according to a systematic, rhythmic, cyclical wholeness.

Yes, God has a plan.

God's plan encompasses not only natural creation, but also the spiritual realm of His created order. And very specifically, His plan involves the spiritual relationship between God and all humanity, including you and me.

God's initial plan was one of intimate, loving, and unbroken fellowship between Himself and His creation. In Genesis 3:8 (NKJV), we read how Adam and Eve "heard the sound of the LORD God walking in the garden in the cool of the day." Adam and Eve knew it was God; apparently, that was a normal activity, a regular part of their day. God created Adam and Eve for His pleasure, so that He might have close communion with them. That has been His desire for humankind from the very beginning. It is His desire today.

The Lord God placed only one limitation on Adam and Eve, that they not eat of one particular tree in the garden—the tree of the knowledge of good and evil. The fact is, God didn't want Adam and Eve to know about evil. He wanted them to know only His goodness and the goodness of what He created for them.

God said about His entire creation, day after day, "It is good." The Garden of Eden was a place of perfection, of God's abiding presence, and of human perfect dominion and leadership of creation. God knew that evil existed, but He had no desire that Adam and Eve know it.

Why did God give Adam and Eve a choice to sin? Because it is choice—the exercise of free will—that separates humankind from the rest of God's earthly creation. All other aspects of God's creation follow the inbred and built-in laws of nature that God established for them. They have no choice to act, respond, or react in ways that are contrary to the way God created them. Humankind is the one aspect of God's creation about which God said, "Let Us make man in Our image" (Gen. 1:26 NKJV). Just as God has free will and can choose how He will respond and what He will initiate, so humankind received this unique ability from God.

God gave Adam and Eve the option of eating from the tree of the knowledge of good and evil because He knew that if they truly were to be creatures of free will, they must have the ability to *choose* to obey Him, to love Him, to fellowship with Him. They needed to have the potential for choosing to obey or disobey. The tree of the knowledge of good and evil wasn't a trick that God placed in their path. Rather, it was a possibility that had to exist if Adam and Eve were to be creatures with free will.

God made it very clear to Adam and Eve that although He was giving them the option, His desire for them—His command to them—was that they *not* eat of the tree. He underscored His command by telling them the consequences of eating from it: "In the day that you eat of it you shall surely die" (Gen. 2:17 NKJV).

Adam and Eve chose to eat of the forbidden tree. And for the first time in their existence, they *knew* evil. They knew what it meant to sin, to feel guilt, to feel spiritually and physically exposed to each other and to God, and to feel unworthy in God's presence. They felt the way that every person after them has felt, and they did what virtually every person has tried to do at some point—they tried to hide from God.

God spelled out the consequences to the serpent that had lied to and tempted Eve, and the consequences to Eve and to Adam. The consequences were just as He had foretold. They were to live from that moment on with hardship—with a knowledge of evil—and with the fate of death. On the day Adam and Eve disobeyed, they began to die. The curse of death was on them. Every day, they would be reminded of their mortality, and especially so through the pain and weariness they felt in their bodies.

God did not act, however, without mercy toward Adam and Eve. He made "tunics of skin, and clothed them" (Gen. 3:21 NKJV). The tunics helped them to face a world that was going to be covered with thorns and thistles. But they also had another meaning.

In making the tunics, God shed blood. Why? Blood is an evidence of life. (See Gen. 9:4.) From the earliest days, humankind recognized that a flow of blood was equated with life. The things that had the pulse of a heartbeat and that were capable of bleeding were things that were different from the land or vegetation in God's creation. God gave Adam and Eve a perpetual reminder—a sign as close to them as their own skin—that He was the Author of *life*, so that even as they walked from the Garden of Eden into a cursed world, with a death sentence on them, they would recognize that God had designed them to *live*. They were always to look to God and remember God as the One who had created them for life.

When Cain and Abel offered sacrifices to God, the blood sacrifice of Abel was acceptable to God. Why? Abel recognized that all life came from God and all life was owed to God. Cain gave to God the fruit of his labor, a gift of his work. It was as if Cain was saying to God, "Look what I've done. Here's a part of my work, given to You." Abel, on the other hand, was saying to God, in effect, "I recognize what You have done and what You alone are capable of doing. You are the Life-giver. I am privileged to be a part of Your work, to tend the sheep that You have given to me."

This message related to life itself is the theme that runs from cover to cover in the Bible. God is the Source of all that gives life and all that is life. God desires that His life be our life. The commandments that God gave to us were intended to spare us from hardship and the ravages of a sinful human heart; they were intended to bring us closer to His heart so that He might shower us with His love and forgiveness. God wants us to acknowledge that we can't make it on our own. We need His life imparted to us in order for us to live day by day. We didn't create ourselves, and we can't sustain ourselves; He alone is God. He alone is Life. Apart from Him, we die—both naturally and spiritually.

God in His Word continually called people to face this reality and turn to Him to receive His love and forgiveness for their sinful state, which they inherited from Adam and Eve. In the Old Testament, God made a provision for relationship to be restored through the sacrifice of animals, especially sheep. The Day of Atonement—a ceremony that brought restoration and reconciliation between God and His people—was all about the shedding of blood, the putting away of sins, the acknowledging of God alone as the Life-giver.

In giving a final challenge to them before they crossed into the land God had promised them, Moses said to the people of Israel,

> *I call heaven and earth as witnesses today against you, that I have set before you life and death, blessing and cursing; therefore choose life, that both you and your descendants may live; that you may love the LORD your God, that you may obey His voice, and that you may cling to Him, for He is your life and the length of your days; and that you may dwell in the land which the LORD swore to your fathers, to Abraham, Isaac, and Jacob, to give them.* (Deut. 30:19–20 NKJV)

God's desire has always been and still is that we choose life! That is His plan.

Jesus said of Himself, "I have come that they may have life, and that they may have it more abundantly" (John 10:10 NKJV). His very purpose for coming to the earth and for dying on the cross was to bring us squarely back to the desire of God's heart from the beginning: God created us to have fellowship with Him and to be in a relationship with Him that is not marred by evil and its resulting rebellion, sin, and separation.

The New Covenant

Do you ever feel distant from God? Do you wonder about your relationship with Him?

God knew that would be the state of the human heart, and He made a provision for a new relationship to be established between Himself and His beloved creation.

In Luke 22:19–20 (NKJV), we read this about Jesus: "And He took bread, gave thanks and broke it, and gave it to them, saying, 'This is My body which is given for you; do this in remembrance of Me.' Likewise He also took the cup after supper, saying, 'This cup is the new covenant in My blood, which is shed for you.'" Jesus was speaking to them about something new that was about to happen— the institution of a new covenant. Jesus came to die for our sins and forgiveness, and as part of His death and resurrection, He established a new life-covenant with humankind.

The Nature of a Covenant

A covenant is a divine agreement between God and humankind. God is the initiator of covenant promises. He is the only One in a position to establish a covenant with us. We can make promises, or vows, to God, but He alone has the authority and prerogative to make covenants with us.

There are about three hundred references to covenants in the Old Testament. Jesus referred to only one covenant in the Gospels: the new covenant described in Luke 22. Covenant was of vital importance to the Jewish people, but covenants throughout God's history with His people changed. The covenant that Jesus established through His death on the cross is a lasting, definitive, and complete covenant. It does not change. It is the covenant God has made with you and me. It is God's plan.

In the Old Testament, God first made a covenant with Noah:

Then God spoke to Noah and to his sons with him, saying, "And as for Me, behold, I establish My covenant with you and with your descendants after you, and with every living creature that is with you: the birds, the cattle, and every beast of the earth with you, of all that go out of the ark, every beast of the earth. Thus I establish My covenant with you: Never again shall all flesh be cut off by the waters of the flood; never again shall there be a flood to destroy the earth." And God said: "This is the sign of the covenant which I make between Me and you,

*and every living creature that is with you, for perpetual gen-
erations: I set My rainbow in the cloud, and it shall be for the
sign of the covenant between Me and the earth. It shall be, when
I bring a cloud over the earth, that the rainbow shall be seen in
the cloud; and I will remember My covenant which is between
Me and you and every living creature of all flesh; the waters
shall never again become a flood to destroy all flesh. The rainbow shall be in the cloud, and I will look on it to remember the
everlasting covenant between God and every living creature of
all flesh that is on the earth." (Gen. 9:8–16 NKJV)*

The Two Types of Covenants

There are two types of covenants. One is a conditional
covenant—in other words, if you do one thing, this is what I will do;
if you do another thing, then this is what I will do. Conditional
covenants hinge upon the behavior of humankind and, very specifically, our willingness to obey God.

The other type is an unconditional covenant. An unconditional
covenant does not depend upon humankind's response. God has
said what He is going to do, and it shall be done, regardless of the
obedience of human beings. The covenant that God made with Noah
was an unconditional covenant. So was His covenant with Abraham
when He said about the land of Canaan: "To your descendants I
have given this land" (Gen. 15:18 NKJV).

In most cases, God established His covenants with the shedding of blood. He did that with Abraham, causing a burning torch
to appear and move among the pieces of the sacrificial offering that
Abraham had made to God. (See Gen. 15:9–17.)

When God gave the Law to Moses, He established the sacrificial system as a means for humankind to enter into relationship
with Him. Hebrews 9:18–20 (NKJV) tells us,

*Therefore not even the first covenant was dedicated without
blood. For when Moses had spoken every precept to all the people according to the law, he took the blood of calves and goats,*

with water, scarlet wool, and hyssop, and sprinkled both the book itself and all the people, saying, "This is the blood of the covenant which God has commanded you."

When Jesus spoke of a new covenant, He spoke of the shedding of blood, and the next day He fulfilled and established this covenant through the sacrifice of His life at Calvary. He became the definitive sacrificial Lamb of God whose blood was shed for the sins of the world.

At the time of Jesus' crucifixion, the veil in the temple tore from top to bottom, opening the way for all people to have direct access to God the Father. Up to that time, only the high priest had direct access to God in the holiest part of the temple, and then, only once a year. Jesus' death made it possible for people's relationship with God to be restored fully, openly, and perpetually.

In the book of Hebrews, we read, "Now He has obtained a more excellent ministry, inasmuch as He is also Mediator of a better covenant, which was established on better promises" (8:6 NKJV). The covenant that Jesus established is better than the old covenant that required continual blood sacrifices. The new covenant is based upon the onetime shedding of Christ's blood.

For if the blood of bulls and goats and the ashes of a heifer, sprinkling the unclean, sanctifies for the purifying of the flesh, how much more shall the blood of Christ, who through the eternal Spirit offered Himself without spot to God, cleanse your conscience from dead works to serve the living God? (Heb. 9:13–14 NKJV)

Jesus has become the *guarantee* or "surety" of this new and better covenant. (See Heb. 7:22.)

The new covenant was foretold by those living under the old covenant, especially the prophet Jeremiah who said,

This is the covenant that I will make with the house of Israel after those days, says the LORD: I will put My law in their minds, and write it on their hearts; and I will be their God, and they shall be My people. . . . I will forgive their iniquity, and their sin I will remember no more. (Jer. 31:33–34 NKJV)

Note especially that we come into accord with God's new covenant not through outer sacrifices, but through inner believing. God's new covenant brings about a change of heart; it is written on our hearts. Those who enter into this covenant know to keep it and want to keep it.

How much can we count on this covenant? Jeremiah also gave us that answer:

Thus says the LORD,
Who gives the sun for a light by day,
The ordinances of the moon and the stars for a light by night,
Who disturbs the sea,
And its waves roar
(The LORD of hosts is His name):
"If those ordinances depart
From before Me, says the LORD,
Then the seed of Israel shall also cease
From being a nation before Me forever."
Thus says the LORD:
"If heaven above can be measured,
And the foundations of the earth searched out beneath,
I will also cast off all the seed of Israel
For all that they have done, says the LORD." (Jer. 31:35–37 NKJV)

God says that His promises are so trustworthy that only if the sun, moon, and stars shoot out of their orbits have we reason to doubt God will remain true to His covenant.

The writer to the Hebrews provided a graphic description of the difference between the old and new covenants. He likened them to two mountains—Sinai, from which the Law of Moses was given, and Zion, the end of which was Calvary on which Christ died:

> *For you have not come to the mountain [Sinai] that may be touched and that burned with fire, and to blackness and darkness and tempest, and the sound of a trumpet and the voice of words, so that those who heard it begged that the word should not be spoken to them anymore. . . . But you have come to Mount Zion and to the city of the living God, the heavenly Jerusalem, to an innumerable company of angels, to the general assembly and church of the firstborn who are registered in heaven, to God the Judge of all, to the spirits of just men made perfect, to Jesus the Mediator of the new covenant, and to the blood of sprinkling that speaks better things than that of Abel.* (Heb. 12:18–24 NKJV)

Our call today is not a call to the old Law of Moses, with its sacrifice of animals, but a call to an acceptance of Christ as the One who brings us into a fully reconciled relationship with God, the Life-giver and the Eternal Life-giver.

God's plan through Christ Jesus is the plan that God has established for us today. Through believing on Him, we have eternal life. Jesus said,

> *For God so loved the world that He gave His only begotten Son, that whoever believes in Him should not perish but have everlasting life. For God did not send His Son into the world to condemn the world, but that the world through Him might be saved.* (John 3:16–17 NKJV)

God's Plan Is One of Grace

When we accept Jesus Christ as Savior, we experience God's grace.

Grace is a word that remains a mystery to many people, including Christians. Here is my definition of grace: *grace is God's kindness and graciousness toward humanity, without regard to worth or merit of those who receive it, and without their deserving it.*

Out of His infinite heart of love, God gives us what we don't deserve and haven't earned. That's grace.

In our sinful nature, we deserve death. We are the heirs of Adam and Eve. We inherited their nature and the consequence of death. We are born with a seed of rebellion in our hearts. We do not live in the perfection of the Garden of Eden; we live in a world that is fallen and in chaos. Death and its forerunners of stress, emotional turmoil, daily toil, pain, disease, hardship, and the wear and tear of aging are common to all of us. We are sinful, and we are deserving of death.

But in God's great love, He has provided a means for us to receive life—to receive what we don't deserve and cannot earn. God sent Jesus to die in our place so that we might live. That's grace!

God's Plan Is Unfolding

Jesus accomplished on the cross everything that needed to be accomplished for the salvation of humankind. There is no more that Jesus needs to do.

On the cross, Jesus defeated the grip of sin on the heart of humankind.

In the Resurrection, Jesus defeated the power of death over humankind.

By His death and resurrection, Jesus defeated the hold that Satan has on humankind.

Why then is humankind still struggling with sin, death, and the influence of Satan? Because humankind as a whole has not accepted what God provided through the sacrificial death and triumphant resurrection of His only begotten Son, Jesus Christ.

God gave. But we, as the whole human race, have not received.

This is true not only on the large scale for all of humanity, but also on the individual scale. Everything that God intends to give us, He gave us the moment we were saved. The full provision was made for our salvation, our eternal life, our wholeness in spirit, mind, and body. God does not parcel out salvation, deliverance, or wholeness to us bit by bit. God makes salvation completely available through Jesus Christ—and not only to specific individuals, but to all who will receive and believe in Jesus Christ as Savior.

Jesus made that very clear by saying, "Whoever believes in Him should not perish but have everlasting life" (John 3:16 NKJV). That word *whoever* includes everybody. No person is excluded from the opportunity to believe and receive everlasting life. Jesus did not say that those who believe would receive a down payment on everlasting life or a promise of everlasting life that they would have to work to fulfill. They receive everlasting life, period.

Why don't we become perfect people instantly upon accepting Christ Jesus? Because we haven't yet matured spiritually to have the capacity for the fullness of His perfection at work in our lives.

Consider a newborn baby. That baby has the full capacity to become a unique and very special adult. All of the genetic code necessary for the baby to grow and develop was given to her even before her birth. There is no more genetic code the baby is going to receive or develop as she grows. Rather, she is going to grow according to the genetic code that is already in place.

The newborn baby has the potential to be able to walk, talk, make decisions and solve problems, decipher fractions, hold a pencil, read a book, give a speech, and display thousands of other skills. But the newborn baby doesn't manifest all of these skills immediately upon birth. Some intellectual skills are developed to coincide with physical maturity; other skills are built upon one another like building blocks. Many skills require the copying of behavior that has been modeled for the growing child, and subsequent practice on the part of the child.

The same is true for us spiritually. God has given us all of the Holy Spirit at the time we receive Jesus Christ as our Savior. We will need to grow up, however, before we will manifest certain traits, spiritual qualities, and spiritual fruit in our lives as spiritually mature individuals.

The grace of God at work in our lives unfolds to us as we are able to experience it. All of God's gifts are deposited into our spiritual account, but as we grow in Christ, we have the ability to access the riches of His glory. It is as if the fullness of God's gifts to us has been put in a trust account on our behalf—just as a parent might set up a trust fund for a child, a fund the child cannot access or spend until he has reached a certain age. The Lord knows not only what we need, but also what we are able to handle.

The Fullness of the Time

In Galatians 4:4, we find the phrase "the fullness of the time." The maturity of the individual seems to be parallel in many ways to the maturity of God's people as a whole. In my ministry, I've seen entire congregations "grow up" over time in their understanding of God's Word and the ways in which they manifest their spiritual maturity in loving outreach to the lost and needy. They reach a place of readiness for God to use them in more dynamic and powerful ways to bless others.

I've also seen this at work in the lives of countless men and women in ministry positions. When I look back on my life, I see this very clearly. As a young pastor in my twenties, I would have had very little ability to do the work of ministry that I do today. I had the energy and the desire to do what I do today, but I didn't have the wisdom, understanding, or depth of compassion then that I have today. That is true for every person I know. God moves us from place to place, from situation to situation, from experience to experience, to "grow us up" so He can use us more.

As long as we are willing to yield to His methods and are willing to grow and change, He will find greater and greater ways to use the talents and abilities that He gave us at our birth, as well as the spiritual gifts and potential in Christ that He gave us at our spiritual birth.

God has a precise timetable for the history of the world. He alone knows when one period in history will end and another will begin. Jesus said of His own return, "Of that day and hour no one knows, not even the angels of heaven, but My Father only" (Matt. 24:36 NKJV).

We can know with certainty that God is working and waiting and watching, always in the process of wooing His children to Himself and of preparing us to receive what He has already prepared for us.

Christ's Sufficiency

What does this mean to us as individuals who are struggling with life's problems?

First, it means that we can take heart that God is at work in us, and He is working through us, to accomplish His purposes. We are a part of His plan. He has a specific role for each of us to fill, and He is developing each of us to fill it.

Second, it means that we need to look only to Christ to prepare us for what is happening and what will happen in this world.

So many people seem concerned these days with the state of the world and with predictions about when Christ will come again. Our primary concern, however, should be with our state of readiness and preparedness for His return. Will we be the people He wants us to be when He comes again?

Jesus told a parable about prayer and faith:

> There was in a certain city a judge who did not fear God nor regard man. Now there was a widow in that city; and she came to him, saying, "Get justice for me from my adversary." And he would not for a while; but afterward he said within himself, "Though I do not fear God nor regard man, yet because this widow troubles me I will avenge her, lest by her continual com-

ing she weary me." . . . *Hear what the unjust judge said. And
shall God not avenge His own elect who cry out day and night
to Him, though He bears long with them? I tell you that He
will avenge them speedily. Nevertheless, when the Son of Man
comes, will He really find faith on the earth?* (Luke 18:2–8
NKJV)

Jesus gave the parable to those who were trusting in themselves
and who felt themselves to be righteous, even though they despised
other people. Certainly, it is a word for us today when so many are
assuming they are "right with God," even though they have never
accepted Jesus as their Savior and are very critical of those who have.

When we look at the state of the world and the future of the
world, we should be reminded to focus on our hearts. When the
Lord looks at us, does He see a people of prayer? Does He see a people of faith?

In making the statement that Christ is our sufficiency, our
total provision, for meeting the challenges of the world today and
tomorrow, I am not denouncing our need for material preparation,
for education, or for living in full accord with God's commandments.
God expects us to live orderly, prudent, and pure lives. I am saying
that we need have no *fear*—and really, very little concern—for what
will happen in the future.

God's plan is His plan. He will execute it according to His
timetable and His methods. We are a part of His plan. We can do
nothing to change God's plan. In fact, the only thing we can do is
to prepare ourselves spiritually for the realization of His plan.

Paul taught the Colossians, "For in Him dwells all the fullness
of the Godhead bodily; and you are complete in Him, who is the
head of all principality and power" (Col. 2:9–10 NKJV).

In Christ, we have the potential for all the preparedness we
need to face, and to withstand, any evil in the world today and any
evil that may come in the future. In Christ, we are made ready, we
are equipped, for any crisis or circumstance that may come. He is
our full security, our complete provision, and our total defense.

I recently heard about a Christian man who had started stockpiling various resources that he felt sure he would need in the coming years because he saw a future filled only with doom and gloom. He believed the world's economy was on the verge of collapse, and he envisioned a life in which he would need to hole up and rely upon his stockpiles of food, water, generators, and other material provisions in order to be able to survive the dark days ahead.

Our defense against evil is not one that we can anticipate fully in the natural or material world. Our only complete defense is in Christ Jesus. He is the only defender against evil that has been or ever will be truly victorious in all situations and circumstances. Jesus said, "Do not labor for the food which perishes, but for the food which endures to everlasting life, which the Son of Man will give you, because God the Father has set His seal on Him" (John 6:27 NKJV).

The children of Israel wandered in a wilderness, but their shoes didn't wear out, even though they wandered there for forty years. When the children of Israel needed water, God supplied it. When they needed food, He sent manna. When they needed guidance, He gave them a very clear and present witness to lead them by day and by night. When they were surrounded by enemies, He delivered them. His means were sovereign and supernatural, and His provision was complete and sure. We can trust the Lord to do the same for us anytime we face evil. Ultimately, there is no defense but the Lord, and only as we trust and obey Him completely are we prepared for what may come our way and for what God will do on our behalf.

We must be ready to move in a moment's time, sensitive to His leading and guidance, quick to respond to His call. That state of readiness and preparedness in the Lord is a mark of spiritual maturity. And God desires that state for His people—both individually and collectively. We must be ready to walk into the fullness of God's plan for the ages and for all humanity at the moment He calls us to act.

God's Method for Fulfilling His Plan

God's foremost method throughout the ages has remained the same. His method for wooing and winning humankind to Himself, and therefore, His method for aligning His people with His plan for the ages, has been love.

God took the initiative in extending this love to us when we were still sinners. He continues to take that initiative day by day as He leads us through the power of the Holy Spirit at work in us. He calls to us in love, saying, "Receive what I have to give to you. Do what I am leading you to do, so I may pour out even more blessings upon you. Speak My words of love to others. Act with love toward those in need. Be My agent for love on this earth. Be the recipient of My great love in your life."

A too prevalent perception of God is one of judgment. Many people I know who are still living in a state of sin regard God as a great judge who is quick to pronounce punishment upon them. Many believers also continue to carry this perception of God in their hearts, even though they have experienced God's forgiveness.

Why is this false perception of God so prevalent?

Because we haven't responded to God's love. We haven't fully opened ourselves to receiving all of the love He longs to pour out toward us.

Have you ever seen a movie or a real-life situation in which a person was about to be hit by someone who was much bigger and much stronger, or who had a huge stick or rod in his hand? The person about to be hit probably cowered and cringed, and perhaps even curled up like a ball in hopes of defending himself as much as possible against the anticipated blows. Many people adopt that position before God. They keep waiting for the blows. If they would only uncurl themselves and look up into the face of their heavenly Father, they would find that God the Father looks exactly like Jesus, His Son. They would find themselves staring into eyes filled with infinite and overflowing love. They would find themselves facing outstretched arms of warm embrace. They would hear words of comfort, affirmation, and encouragement.

Our inability to experience God's love is much like our inability to experience the fullness of God's power working in us; we haven't yielded ourselves to His love. We have closed ourselves to God and put up a DO NOT TOUCH, DO NOT ENTER, DO NOT TRESPASS sign against Him.

That doesn't keep God from loving us. He continues to love and to love and to love. He will send His love to us in any way He can find to send it.

I heard about a woman who became the foster mother for a child who had been badly abused. The four-year-old boy threw terrible temper tantrums the minute any adult tried to come close to him. He refused to be touched or held and became stiff as a board anytime his foster mother or foster father picked him up.

This woman said, "One day I went into this child's room and closed the door behind me and said to myself, 'I'm not leaving until I have a breakthrough with this child.' No sooner had I closed the door behind me than Buddy began to run furiously around the room, yelling at the top of his lungs, even though I sat calmly in a chair and didn't make a move either toward him or away from him. He finally collapsed into a whimper in the corner of the room, where he curled up into a little ball and covered his head with his hands and arms, as if to ward off what he thought were going to be blows. I didn't move. I continued to sit in my chair and to say softly to him, 'Buddy, I love you. I'm not going to hurt you. I love you. I'm not going to hurt you.'

"It took a long time before Buddy opened his eyes and began to peer out from under one arm to see what I was going to do. More minutes passed. When he saw that I hadn't moved and that I hadn't changed my message—I was still saying, 'Buddy, I love you. I'm not going to hurt you'—he uncurled his little body and sat staring at me from the corner. When he did that, I got up and left the room quietly.

"I repeated this for two more days. Each day Buddy went through the same routine of running and yelling, but for shorter periods of time. On the fourth day, I took a large doll with me into the room and cuddled it as I sat in the chair talking in soothing tones to Buddy. I continued to say, 'I love you, Buddy. I'm not going to hurt you.' I also added, 'Wouldn't you like to come and sit with my doll and me?'

"By the seventh day, Buddy had decided that he'd like to sit with my doll and me. He allowed me to pick him up and hold him, stroking his hair and talking gently to him. He was still stiff as a board in my arms, but at least he allowed me to hold him. By the tenth day, he finally relaxed fully in my arms and actually went to sleep while I gently rocked him.

"I've never had a foster parenting experience that moved me more deeply. Buddy was with us for almost three years before he was adopted by a family who has loved him greatly during the last several years. Best of all, Buddy was ready to receive their love and give them his love. He had learned to trust other people to love him, and over those three years with us, he also learned that those who love also chastise, but that they never abuse."

Is God calling to you today, "I love you; I'm not going to hurt you"? His method for reaching out to you is love. His method for perfecting you is love. The form His love takes may appear to be chastisement, but it is never abuse. His love molds you; it doesn't break you.

God is not out to destroy you, but to woo you to Himself. His desire is not to destroy the world, but to win the world.

God's plan is one for ultimate good. Paul wrote to the Romans about God's redemptive plan for all creation,

I consider that the sufferings of this present time are not worthy to be compared with the glory which shall be revealed in us. For the earnest expectation of the creation eagerly waits for the revealing of the sons of God. For the creation was subjected to futility, not willingly, but because of Him who subjected it in hope;

because the creation itself also will be delivered from the bondage
of corruption into the glorious liberty of the children of God.
(Rom. 8:18–21 NKJV)

God has a plan for the full redemption of us as individuals, for all humankind, and for all creation. It is a plan that moves us from corruption to purity, from bondage to liberty.

Once you catch sight of God's plan and uncurl yourself to receive God's love and to participate in God's purposes, you can't help experiencing hope. You'll find that you are quick to say,

---

I have hope because God has a master plan for good for all His creation and I am a part of it, now and every day to come.

CHAPTER 3

GOD HAS A PERSONALIZED BLUEPRINT FOR YOU

When Tom came to my office, he was the picture of dejection and discouragement. His shoulders were slumped over; his head was down. I stood as straight as I could in hopes that he might stand a little straighter too. It didn't work. When he sat down, he sat down with a slump.

As Tom told me his story, I found myself thinking again and again, *He's tired. Whipped, beaten down, trampled*—all of those might have been good terms to describe the man in my office. Tom was weary to the very core of his being.

And he knew it. He said, "Pastor, I've been working hard. I'm putting in long hours on the job. My boss seems to think that anybody who puts in only fifty hours a week isn't doing enough, so I'm working about sixty hours a week. I've volunteered for several things here at the church, and my wife and kids are complaining that they never see me. I missed my little girl's piano recital last week, and last month I missed an important football game in which my son scored a touchdown. I feel that I'm not doing enough on any front, but I just don't see how I can do more. I came to you today to ask you what I should do—how I can fit it all in and keep juggling everything I'm doing. You do a lot of different things, but you don't seem stressed out as I am."

"I've been there," I said to him. "I know what it means to overextend yourself."

"You do?" he asked.

"Sure I do," I said. "I've been there in my life." And then I added, "I can tell you're working hard, Tom. But let me ask you this: *Why* are you working so hard?"

"Well," he said, "to keep my job, for one thing, and to be in a position at work so I can get promoted and get ahead. I have a wife and two children who are counting on me."

"Why are you working so hard at church?"

"Because I think it's important to work for God," he said.

"Did God ask you to take on these various volunteer positions?" I asked him.

He paused for a moment and then said, "I don't know what you mean. Doesn't God *want* me to be active at church?"

I said, "He wants you to do the things He asks you to do. He wants you to obey Him. But lots of times we don't ask God first exactly what He wants us to do. We go ahead and volunteer and then ask Him later to help us when we're so tired, we can hardly move."

"That's true," Tom said. "I never thought to ask God if I should take on these committees and responsibilities. I just jumped right in because I thought it was the right thing to do."

I suggested to Tom that he spend some time in prayer asking God how God desired for him to spend his time. "Do what God impresses on your heart to do. He may want you to change some of your priorities, and that may mean dropping some things. He may want you to keep doing what you're doing and ask you to trust Him to give you the strength and energy you need."

I didn't feel, however, as if Tom and I had arrived at the real reason he was in my office. I asked him, "Tom, how do you think God feels about you?"

Tom seemed surprised at my question. "I know that God has forgiven me and that I'm a Christian," he said. "Is that what you mean?"

"That's part of it," I said. "But how do you think God feels about you right now? What's His opinion of you?"

"I don't think He necessarily likes how tired I am," he said. "He probably doesn't approve of how much time I spend away from my wife and kids."

"But how does He feel about *you*?" I pressed.

"God loves me?" Tom said with a question mark. "Is that what you're getting at?"

"Closer," I said. "Do you think that God approves of *you*—who you are as a person? Do you think that He likes you, that He likes spending time with you?"

"I never really thought about that," Tom said. "I think He might approve of some things in my life, but there's a lot of room for improvement. There's a lot more God would probably like for me to be doing."

"Like what?" I said. "It sounds to me as if you already have your schedule filled to the maximum."

"Well," he said, "I could spend more time praying and studying my Bible. I could witness more about Christ."

"And do you think God would like you better if you did those things?"

"Yeah, probably," Tom said.

"I don't think it would change His opinion about you at all," I said.

Tom seemed very surprised. "You don't?" he asked.

"No, I think God loves you as much as He can possibly love you. And along with His love comes total unconditional acceptance of you. He *loves* you, Tom, but He also likes you. You are His child.

He doesn't like it when you sin because sin hurts you, and He doesn't want to see you hurt. Anytime you sin, He stands ready with open arms to forgive you. He likes being with you. He likes talking to you and listening to you. He likes doing things for you."

I could tell from the expression on his face that nobody had ever told Tom that before.

"You really think so?" he asked softly.

"Yes," I said. "I really think so. God can't save you any more than He has already saved you. When Jesus died on the cross to make it possible for you to receive God's forgiveness, He *died*. There's no more dying required. When Jesus rose from the dead, He *rose*. What Jesus did for you is completed. You were fully justified before God the moment you accepted Jesus as your Savior. You were fully forgiven the moment you asked for God's forgiveness. There's no more justifying to do. There's nothing else you need to do to earn God's approval or win His approval."

"I never thought about it like that," Tom said.

"Most people don't. The fact is, Tom, that many people I meet are still trying to do something to win God's approval. They are still trying to earn a little bit of what God has already freely given to them."

"Do you think I've been trying to earn God's approval?" Tom asked sincerely.

"I don't know," I said. "I think it's a possibility. The assurance I want to give you today is that God approves of you, Tom, whether you work sixty hours a week or forty hours a week. God approves of you whether you volunteer for six committees or no committees. God loves you and He approves of you on the basis of what Jesus did for you, not on the basis of what you are trying to do for Jesus."

"But doesn't God want us to work for the church?" Tom asked.

"God desires that we respond to Him out of love and devotion. Our motivation in serving others is to be solely because we love God, not because we think we have to do certain good works to please God. When you love a person, you are quick to see what you can do to show that person how much you love her or him. That's far different from doing things for a person so that the other person might approve of you, like you, or love you. The same is true for your relationship with God. He already loves you, likes you, and approves of you. Nothing you can do will change that. Knowing that God already approves of you fully should free you to do what you want to do or what you feel led by the Holy Spirit to do. There shouldn't be anything that you feel you have to do to win God's approval."

"I can see the difference," Tom said. "I think I have some praying to do . . . and then some decisions to make."

I saw Tom again a few weeks later after a church function he had helped to organize. "How are things going?" I asked.

"Great!" he said. He had a smile on his face and a bounce to his step. He was standing tall and straight. "I had that talk with God," he said, "and I felt I should drop one of the things I was doing."

I nodded. "That sounds right," I said.

"But the amazing thing, Pastor, is that I really didn't want to stop doing any of the other things. I just changed my attitude toward them. I decided I would volunteer only if I felt that the task was a way I could express my love to God—not for any other reason. And suddenly, things began to go more smoothly. I got a lot more done in the same amount of time. I felt more fulfillment in what I was doing. I found a way to involve my wife and kids in a couple of the things I had volunteered to do, and we're having a great time as a family doing these activities. God and I are having a great time together."

"I can see that!" I said. "Remember, Tom. God likes you."

"I know that," Tom said with a big smile on his face. "I really *know* that."

God Approves of You

I never thought much about whether God liked me or approved of me when I was a teenager or young man. I knew based upon Scripture that God loved me, but I never thought about whether He liked me. If I had been pressed on that point, I probably would have concluded that God somewhat liked me. I don't think I would have said that He liked me through and through.

It was only after I truly experienced God's love—His total, unconditional, overwhelming abundant love—that I came to the place in my life where I could say with all honesty, "Yes, God likes me. He approves of me. He likes spending time with me. He likes being with me. He likes hearing me when I talk to Him, and He likes talking back to me through His Word. God thinks I'm OK."

I didn't come to that position on the basis of things I had accomplished or actions I had taken. Rather, I came to that position solely because I had a new appreciation for God's grace at work in my life. The fact is, there was nothing I had done, or could ever do, that would win God's approval. God likes me just the way I am because He created me to be just the way I am. He likes my personality because He created my personality.

God's approval of me isn't based on anything I have done or might do. He approves of me because I stand forgiven before Him. I'm forgiven because I have accepted Jesus Christ as my Savior and have received God's forgiveness. That makes me totally acceptable to Him.

The first four chapters of Romans make it very clear that we can't save ourselves. We are all sinners and have fallen short of the glory of God. (See Rom. 3:23.) But because of what Jesus Christ did for us on the cross, we are "justified freely by His grace" (Rom. 3:24 NKJV).

Jesus has done for you what you cannot do. He won for you God's full approval. You cannot have grace without the Cross. But because of the Cross, you have full access to God's grace.

Grace is God's kindness and graciousness toward you *without regard to worth or merit*. You can't earn grace, you can't buy grace, and you can't barter with God to receive grace. It is a free gift of God to you. There is only one thing you can do related to grace, and that is to receive grace.

Trying to Win God's Approval

Are you trying to win God's approval? Many people have that tendency, especially if they grew up with an inferiority complex.

I grew up not experiencing much in the way of approval. I remember only two people in my life, other than my mom, who registered any signs of approval of me during my growing-up years. One was a schoolteacher named Mrs. Ferrell, whom I overheard saying to another teacher, "I like Charles." Those three simple words meant something to me!

The other person who showed me that he approved of me was a Sunday school teacher named Craig Stowe. He came down to the street corner to buy newspapers from me even though he had the newspaper delivered to his home—just to encourage me. Mrs. Ferrell and Mr. Stowe were like beacons in a wilderness of disapproval that I experienced at school and at home.

My stepfather repeatedly gave me the message that I wasn't good for anything, wasn't worth anything, and would never amount to anything. Numerous teachers and other adults sent me the message that I was a failure and had little hope for a bright future.

A child who grows up in that kind of environment tends to do one of two things: give up on life, or try extra hard to prove to somebody that he is worthy of something. I took the second path.

I studied hard in college and then in seminary to prove that I was worthy. When I became a pastor, I poured myself into my pastoral duties, always seeking to do far more than what was required to win the approval of others, including God. I drove myself and those who worked alongside me. I ended up physically exhausted and emotionally feeling empty.

If you are trying to do something to win God's approval, the question you must ask yourself is this: How much is enough?

How much prayer is enough prayer? How much Bible reading is enough Bible reading? On how many committees at church do you need to work to be on enough committees? How much good work do you need to do to qualify for enough good work?

The reality is, you can never do enough. Just when you think that you've done enough, guilt and feelings of inferiority and a need for approval will rear up and say, "You've got to do more." There is no end.

You can never do enough to thank God for sending Jesus to the cross. You can never do enough good works to equal what Jesus Christ did in dying for your sins. You can never do enough to compensate Jesus for His sacrifice on your behalf.

Now, all those years when I was working hard to prove myself worthy, if you had asked me, "Is God's grace free?" I would have answered with a resounding, "Yes, God's grace is free."

If you had asked, "Is God's forgiveness free?" I would have said, "Yes, it's free to me." God's forgiveness cost the life of Jesus, but to me, His forgiveness is given freely.

If you had questioned why I was working so hard, I probably would have told you that I was working hard because it was my nature to work hard or perhaps because I always tried to do my best. Both facts are truthful, but they don't tell the whole truth. Part of me was trying to thank God for saving me; I was trying to do something for Him because He had done so much for me. It was a tendency, although an unconscious one, to try to pay God back for my salvation.

When I fully experienced God's love in my life, I had a new perspective on grace. I was able to relax in the fact that God was extending to me the fullness of His grace. I could obtain no more grace. Christ Jesus purchased it all for me. My role was one of receiving, of thanksgiving, of loving God with my whole heart. There was nothing I needed to do. There was nothing else I could do. It had all been done for me.

Why does someone continue to strive to win more of God's approval through good works?

First, old habits. Anytime you do something for God because you think you *should* do it in order for God to like you better, love you more, or approve of you more highly, think again. That's an old habit. That's part of old-creature thinking. That's not a part of what Jesus obtained for you on the cross.

If you are trying to pay God back for saving you, then you haven't accepted or received His grace.

If you are doing good works in order to put yourself into a position to deserve eternal life, then you haven't accepted God's grace. The only means to obtain eternal life is to believe in Jesus Christ as God's atoning sacrifice on your behalf.

If you are trying to suffer for your sins in order to be worthy of salvation, then you haven't accepted God's grace. Suffering for sins is a form of purgatory; Jesus came to deliver you from that form of suffering.

If you are confessing your sins again and again and again in hopes that God might hear you and forgive you, then you haven't accepted God's grace. You don't win forgiveness because of confession. The Cross made forgiveness possible.

There is nothing, nothing, nothing you can do to win or deserve or prove yourself worthy of God's love and grace toward you. There is nothing you can do to make God love you any more than He already loves you.

Created for Good Works, Not Saved by Good Works

One of the great verses in the Bible about God's love and grace is Ephesians 2:10 (NKJV): "We are His workmanship, created in Christ Jesus for good works, which God prepared beforehand that we should walk in them." Perhaps no other verse in the Bible so succinctly and clearly tells you that God sees you as a precious person.

Note, however, that you are God's *workmanship*. The word in the Greek language in which the verse was written means "a person of notable excellence." God calls you a person of notable excellence because He made you. There is no other reason. It has nothing to do with whether you look excellent, act excellent, or do excellent things. You are a prized example of His creation.

As a Christian, your creation is fulfilled in Christ Jesus. This is actually a rebirth or a re-creation of you. Paul wrote, "If anyone is in Christ, he is a new creation; old things have passed away; behold, all things have become new" (2 Cor. 5:17 NKJV). When you become a new creation in Christ Jesus, God expects you to get rid of the old creation—the old messages about your sins and inabilities, incapacities, and inferiority. He expects you to think and act like a new person because His Holy Spirit is now residing within you to help you think and act like a new person.

This isn't a matter of awakening one morning and looking at yourself in the mirror and saying, "I'm going to do things differently. I'm going to succeed." Rather, it's a matter of saying to God every morning, "I'm Yours. I accept by faith that Your Holy Spirit now resides in me. I am trusting You to lead me to act and think as Jesus would act and think. Help me to live Your life today."

Christ does the re-creating in you. You don't do it. It is His work. And because it is His work, and His alone, you cannot boast about your good works. The fact is, they are *His* works.

Every other religion operates on the basis of works—follow a certain ritual, complete a certain list of required things, and you have "arrived." Christianity says that nothing you do can earn you favor with God.

Consider these verses:

Not by works of righteousness which we have done, but according to His mercy He saved us, through the washing of regeneration and renewing of the Holy Spirit, whom He poured out on us abundantly through Jesus Christ our Savior, that having been justified by His grace we should become heirs according to the hope of eternal life. (Titus 3:5–7 NKJV)

Share with me in the sufferings for the gospel according to the power of God, who has saved us and called us with a holy calling, not according to our works, but according to His own purpose and grace which was given to us in Christ Jesus. (2 Tim. 1:8–9 NKJV)

If Abraham was justified by works, he has something to boast about, but not before God. For what does the Scripture say? "Abraham believed God, and it was accounted to him for righteousness." Now to him who works, the wages are not counted as grace but as debt. But to him who does not work but believes on Him who justifies the ungodly, his faith is accounted for righteousness. (Rom. 4:2–5 NKJV)

Works do not add up to salvation. Rather, Christ Jesus saved you in order to do good. He is the One who enables you to do good works. He is their author and their motivation.

The most challenging person to lead to Christ, in my experience, is the "good person." Such a person believes, *I haven't done anything wrong so I don't need forgiveness. I do good things, and God will reward me.*

Such a person believes in the heart of hearts that God is motivated by our good works to save us. The exact opposite is true. God saves us so that we might be motivated to do good works. When it comes to having a desire to do good works, God pours it out. We don't pump it up.

Holy living doesn't put us into a position to receive God's love and forgiveness. Rather, God's love and forgiveness become our motivation for holy living. We no longer have a desire to do anything that might hurt the heart of the Lord who has loved us so completely and so lavishly.

Your Acceptance of God's Grace and Your Destiny

What do God's love and forgiveness have to do with your personal destiny?

Everything!

God's plan for your life is that you might be in close fellowship with Him. The means of having that close fellowship is accepting Jesus Christ as your Savior. In accepting Jesus Christ, you are receiving God's forgiveness and opening yourself up to His love.

That's your number one reason for living on this earth—to love God back. That is the foremost aspect of the destiny God has for you!

Once you have received God's forgiveness for your sinful nature and have received God's gift of the Holy Spirit poured out into your spirit, then you are ready to fulfill the rest of God's plan for your life, which is this: to follow the Lord wherever He leads you. Your destiny will unfold before you as you obey the daily prompting and leading and guiding of the Holy Spirit.

Where Will God Lead?

I don't know all the details about where God will lead you. Only God knows that, and He rarely gives any of us the complete picture of our future. However, God has at least three things as a destiny for each person who has accepted Jesus Christ as Savior and who is seeking to follow Him as Lord.

First, your destiny is to know God's Word.

Time and again, I hear new believers in Christ say, "I have a great desire to read the Bible." When people come to know Christ, they have a desire to know Him better, and the best way to know Him is to read about Him and to read what He had to say.

Those who don't read their Bibles are subject to what Paul described as "every wind of doctrine, by the trickery of men, in the cunning craftiness of deceitful plotting" (Eph. 4:14 NKJV). On the other hand, those who know the Bible reap the benefits described here: "All Scripture is given by inspiration of God, and is profitable for doctrine, for reproof, for correction, for instruction in righteousness, that the man [or woman] of God may be complete, thoroughly equipped for every good work" (2 Tim. 3:16–17 NKJV).

Those who come to Christ not only have a new thirst to read the Bible, but also have a new ability to understand it. One woman described her experience this way: "Before I came to Christ, the Bible was a great mystery to me. I'd read it and think, *What does that say?* After I came to Christ, it was as if somebody had tampered with my Bible. Suddenly, I read it and it made sense. The truth of God seemed to leap off the page and right into my mind."

Regularly reading the Bible offers several advantages to you:

You know what God expects. You don't have to wonder about God's opinion or question whether your behavior is pleasing or displeasing to God.

You are available to God so that God can speak to you. The foremost way that God communicates with you on a regular basis is through His Word. His Word is as timely and applicable to your life today as it was on the day it was first written into words. God's opinion hasn't changed and won't change. What He said in centuries past is true for you now.

Sometimes when I read my Bible, certain words, phrases, or verses seem to leap off the page. They stand out as if they are in bold type, with letters two feet high. I find myself saying, "Why didn't I see *that* before?" I know God is bringing something to my attention that is important for me to know.

As many times as I have read my entire Bible, I still have new insights into God's Word every time I sit down to read it. The Bible is always fresh; it never grows stale. Often I find that God leads me to read a particular passage just when I need it the most. He reminds me of what I already know so that I will be able to use His truth in a very specific way in the hours or days ahead.

The wonder of God's Word is that you can never understand it fully. God's Word holds countless layers of insight and meaning, and it is applicable in unique ways to an infinite number of situations. The more you grow in your relationship with God, the more insights you have into His character and into the way in which God operates. You have a growing understanding of who you are created to be and called to be.

I heard of a woman who was invited to attend a Sunday school class on the Bible, and she responded by saying, "Oh, I don't need that. I've already read the Bible." She didn't know what she was missing! To have read the Bible one time from cover to cover is not enough—far from it. In saying what she did, the woman put herself into that unfortunate category of people who don't know what they don't know.

Although God's Word is always fresh and timely, and always uniquely applicable to the very situation you are facing, God's Word is always sure and absolute. It doesn't change when the cultural norms shift or the traditions of a society change. Neither does the Bible contradict itself. It holds the fundamental truth of life that spans every generation, every culture, every relationship, and every condition of the human heart. You can count on the Bible to be true every moment of the rest of your life.

You have a knowledge base that God can tap at any hour of the day or night. God brings His Word to your remembrance in very timely ways—right at the moment when you need to make a decision, encourage another person, or solve a problem. Unless you have planted God's Word in your mind, He can't bring it to your remembrance.

There have been times when I have gone to bed with a problem on my mind and God has awakened me in the middle of the night with a verse of Scripture running through my mind. At other times, I awaken in the morning with a particular verse as my first thought of the day. I know God is bringing to my remembrance the Word that I have already planted in my mind; He is speaking to me very directly His advice on the matter that has been troubling me.

Reading the Bible regularly also gives you a head start on Bible study, particularly study directed toward solving problems and making decisions.

Countless times when I have faced a particular problem or difficult situation in my life, God has called me to a deeper study of His Word. Such a study is beyond my regular reading of the Bible. I get out reference books and spend hour after hour searching God's Word for the wisdom and understanding that I need and that I know God desires for me to have. Sometimes this study is completed in one session; sometimes this study spans several days, even weeks.

As I study, God will bring to mind a passage or verse of Scripture that is critical to the understanding He wants me to have, but that I would not otherwise have thought to look up or read. When we read and study the Bible regularly, it is as if we are giving God a full keyboard of notes on which He can play for us His new song of wisdom.

You begin to see the big picture of what God desires for His people to be, say, and do. Unless you are reading the Bible regularly, and reading in all sections of the Bible, you will not have a grasp of the whole of God's Word. The error in not reading all of God's Word is that you may begin to emphasize one aspect of God's commandments or promises and become out of balance in doctrine.

Heresies and false teaching nearly always begin the same way: a person finds one small segment of God's Word that he likes, and he pulls that teaching out of context and exalts it as a greater truth than the rest of God's Word. The things that we like in God's Word, of course, are the passages that we interpret as meeting our desire for immediate self-gratification or satisfying our emotional and physical appetites. If we are reading only the parts of God's Word that we *like*, we are probably missing out on the very aspects of God's Word that we *need*. It's vitally important to a balanced Christian walk that we read the whole of God's Word.

You experience an ongoing renewal of your mind. Paul urged, "Do not be conformed to this world, but be transformed by the renewing of your mind, that you may prove what is that good and acceptable and perfect will of God" (Rom. 12:2 NKJV).

As you read God's Word regularly, the Holy Spirit uses what you read to change the thought patterns of your mind. You begin to respond to life as Christ Jesus responded. The Scriptures become the foundation for your attitudes and beliefs, which in turn govern your behavior.

Paul referred to the sanctification (the setting apart) of the believers as occurring "with the washing of water by the word" (Eph. 5:26 NKJV). The more you read God's Word, the more it cleanses your mind of sinful thoughts and desires. Your thought life is cleaned up. You begin to desire in your mind what God desires for you. You no longer think as the world thinks, and as a result, you no longer talk or act as the world talks and acts.

I heard about a young man who accepted Christ while he was attending a university graduate school about a hundred miles from home. His Christian parents were thrilled when he called home to say that he had accepted Christ and had started to read his Bible regularly. His parents noted change after change in him. Every time he came home they noticed something new about him. His appearance changed. He no longer sprinkled his comments with profanity. His taste in music, movies, and books changed. He made new friends. He stopped smoking and drinking. He became more responsible in his spending habits.

His parents never said a word to him about any of those things, although they had deplored much of his past behavior and were delighted with every change they saw in him. They wisely recognized that God was doing a sovereign work in his life. The changes were not a matter of what people had suggested or advised; the changes were ones that the Holy Spirit had prompted directly in the young man's heart. The young man was being transformed by the renewal of his mind.

God's Word changes us. That's one thing that separates the Bible from any other book ever written. The more we read it, the more we are transformed as the Holy Spirit takes God's Word and implants it into our minds and hearts.

God desires for every believer in Christ Jesus to be changed in this way. His destiny for you personally may not be that you become a Bible teacher or a professor of Bible, but God's destiny for you is certainly that you know His Word and that you continually grow in your understanding of His Word.

Second, your destiny is to keep God's commandments.

Part of your destiny is to live in a godly manner on a day-to-day basis in the culture and locale where God has placed you.

Knowing God's Word is a prerequisite to knowing God's commandments. God's rules for living are not limited to the Ten Commandments or to the first five books of the Bible called the Law. The entire Bible is a manual for how God desires that we live our lives. It is God's message to us of what He considers to be right and wrong. It is always God's desire for His people to keep His commandments—to say, do, and be what is good and right in His sight.

Once you have accepted Christ as your Savior, you embark on a new way of living. Most people I know say that when they come to know Christ, they feel new inside. There's a freshness, a cleansing, a good feeling of starting over—just as Jesus said, it is a feeling of being "born again." From God's perspective, this newness of life means that you have been cleansed so that you might live in a way that is different from your sinful past. This new way of living is fully in keeping with God's commandments.

I heard about a Jewish man who had accepted Christ as the Messiah. The man had been raised in what he termed an "unreligious" home, although his parents had taken him to the synagogue as a child to receive instruction in the Law of Moses. He had known from the time he was a child what God considered to be right and wrong behavior. Even so, he said, "Once I accepted Christ, I discovered that I could no longer do all sorts of things that I once had considered to be a normal part of life. Again and again, I was confronted by the Holy Spirit, who spoke in my spirit, *This is not right for you to do or say*. I thought I knew the Ten Commandments. I discovered that I may have known them, but I had never really thought about the Ten Commandments as being a way that I personally was supposed to live. I knew them as historical, literary, even theological fact, but not as a living reality in my personal life. After I came to Christ, I saw that God had a very specific way that I was supposed to live every day, and it was a way that was totally in keeping with His Law and, in many ways, totally contradictory to the way the culture as a whole and my particular social group had said to live."

New Testament Only?

Many people today call themselves New Testament Christians. Part of what they seem to mean in calling themselves this is that they no longer believe the Old Testament has any application to their lives. Jesus said,

> *Do not think that I came to destroy the Law or the Prophets. I did not come to destroy but to fulfill. For assuredly, I say to you, till heaven and earth pass away, one jot or one tittle will by no means pass from the law till all is fulfilled. Whoever therefore breaks one of the least of these commandments, and teaches*

*men so, shall be called least in the kingdom of heaven; but who-
ever does and teaches them, he shall be called great in the kingdom of heaven. For I say to you, that unless your righteousness
exceeds the righteousness of the scribes and Pharisees, you will
by no means enter the kingdom of heaven.* (Matt. 5:17–20 NKJV)

Jesus was calling His followers to live according to the *spirit* of
the Law, which transcends the *letter* of the Law. Again and again in
the Sermon on the Mount, Jesus said, "You have heard that it was
said to those of old." He then cited a traditional teaching of the Law,
but moved on immediately to say, "But I say to you"—and He then
gave a teaching that called for compliance with the spirit or the true
meaning underlying the statements of the Law.

For example, Jesus said, "You have heard that it was said to
those of old, 'You shall not murder, and whoever murders will be in
danger of the judgment.' But I say to you that whoever is angry with
his brother without a cause shall be in danger of the judgment"
(Matt. 5:21–22 NKJV).

Jesus went beyond the letter of the Old Testament commandments to call His disciples into not only keeping the commandments, but also desiring to keep the commandments. He called upon
them to fulfill the spirit of the Law.

Now, Jesus fulfilled the laws of the Old Testament regarding
sacrifices. He became the one complete, substitutionary, and all-sufficient sacrifice for sin when He was crucified on the cross. We are
no longer under the old blood covenant; we are under the new blood
covenant that was instituted when Jesus' blood was shed on the cross.
Therefore, we no longer are required to sacrifice animals or to make
sacrifices of incense, grain, or wine. Rather, we celebrate the fact
that Jesus Himself was our sacrifice for sin every time we partake
of the Communion elements in the Lord's Supper.

The Old Testament laws governing human behavior and
human relationships, however, are just as applicable to us today
as they were to the Israelites four thousand years ago. The Law as
a whole provides a framework for our loving God and loving our

neighbors as ourselves. (See Matt. 22:37–40.) To be a Christian means to take just as seriously the teachings of the Old Testament as the teachings of the New Testament.

The wonderful benefit to being a New Testament Christian is that God has added a "want to" to the "have to" regarding His commandments. The Holy Spirit dwelling within us convicts, prompts, leads, and inspires us to want to follow God with all of the heart, mind, and soul. We want to do what is pleasing to God. We want to live in a daily relationship with Him that is not marred by sin. The Holy Spirit compels us to want more of God's presence operational in and throughout our lives. Our desire is to do what is right.

Our lives are to become living expressions of the commandments of God. In other words, people should be able to read our behavior and know what God considers to be right and wrong. In 2 Corinthians 3:3 (NKJV), we read, "Clearly you are an epistle of Christ . . . written not with ink but by the Spirit of the living God, not on tablets of stone but on tablets of flesh, that is, of the heart."

Believers and unbelievers alike should be able to look at us and see the gospel being applied continuously to real-life situations. Our lives should be of such high moral behavior and of such consistency that others should have no difficulty in determining what we believe and whom we follow.

License to Sin?

Some people seem to think that once they have accepted Jesus Christ as Savior, they are immune from any consequences for sin. Some take their salvation as a "license" to sin. The thinking seems to be, *I can sin, and since I've accepted Christ, I won't go to hell.*

Salvation is not a license to sin, but a call to righteousness. Those who have been genuinely born again have no *desire* to sin. They know they have been saved from a nature that is prone to sin, and they have no desire to return to that state. They know they were in darkness and separated from God. Having experienced the light of Christ, they have no desire to return to darkness. When I hear of a person who claims he is immune from sin's discipline and, there-fore, won't face any consequences for sinful behavior, I question whether that person ever truly experienced salvation. The saved person doesn't want to sin.

The Scriptures assure us repeatedly that once a person has turned to God and accepted His forgiveness for her sin nature, she is transformed by the power of the Holy Spirit into a new creature—one who bears a nature like that of Christ Jesus. The saved person has been thoroughly cleansed and, even beyond that, changed spir-itually. God's Holy Spirit indwells that person from the moment of salvation, and the Holy Spirit never departs from her.

The assurance of our salvation is the steadfastness, trustwor-thiness, and faithfulness of God Himself. He does not come and go from our lives. Once we invite Him to come into our spirits with His saving, transforming love, He is with us to stay. He never departs from us. We have God's promise: "I will never leave you nor forsake you" (Heb. 13:5 NKJV).

The presence of the Holy Spirit within us continues to convict us in an ongoing way as a means of leading us away from sin and toward the righteousness of God. We feel His prompting and nudg-ing in our spirits, calling us to make right choices and good deci-sions—to resist temptation and to stand strong against evil. The Holy Spirit is like an inner antenna that helps us to receive and tune in continually God's will for our lives.

When we override the convicting power of the Holy Spirit and harden our consciences against Him, He frequently turns up the volume of His message. Those who continue to choose sin over righ-teousness sometimes become downright miserable; they are con-fronted at every turn with what they know to be right. The Holy Spirit acts with increasing power to keep us from sin.

Why? Because sin always bears evil consequences. We may not experience the consequences immediately, or even in a short-range period, but we will experience them eventually. We cannot sin with-out experiencing the consequences of sin, which ultimately are deadly. God never winks at sin; He never overlooks it or lets it slide by. Those who persist in sin without seeking God's forgiveness or turning away from sin in repentance will eventually reap its harvest. The Scriptures tell us very plainly:

> *Do not be deceived, God is not mocked; for whatever a man sows, that he will also reap. For he who sows to his flesh will of the flesh reap corruption, but he who sows to the Spirit will of the Spirit reap everlasting life.* (Gal. 6:7–8 NKJV)

> *Sow the wind, and reap the whirlwind.* (Hos. 8:7 NKJV)

Anytime you recognize that you are engaging in sin, you need to turn immediately to the Lord and ask for His forgiveness and His help in changing your ways. This is the way to keep the conscience clear and in good working order. The person who continually ignores the whispering of the Holy Spirit in the inner spirit will develop a hard heart, which includes a deadened conscience.

Third, your destiny is to be a witness for Jesus Christ on the earth.

Every Christian is called to an active ministry. That does not mean that every Christian is called to be a full-time pastor, preacher, or evangelist. It does mean that every Christian is called to share the gospel with other people by what he or she says and does, and to do so under the leadership of the Holy Spirit.

Your destiny as a follower of Jesus Christ is to ask the Lord daily to guide your steps so that you walk precisely where Jesus would walk if He were in your shoes. Your destiny is to be sensitive to His leading and to act when He says to act, and *not* to act when He calls upon you to wait or to be silent.

Years ago we were facing a real need at In Touch Ministries to expand. We found a piece of property that seemed to be right—the price of the property was high, but fair. Members of our executive staff were in agreement that the property was right for us.

Every time I prayed about buying that property, however, I felt God speaking in my spirit, *Don't do that.* I told the staff, "We aren't going to buy that property." I asked them to pray specifically about the purchase of that property, and as they prayed, God revealed the same message to them. In the end, God led us to an even better piece of property, and He sovereignly provided the money with which to buy it.

The leading of the Holy Spirit is very practical. Throughout the Scriptures, we have examples of the Lord saying to various ones, "Do this, do that. Go here, go there." The leading of the Holy Spirit is also leading that results in a win-win proposition for everybody involved. The devil is the only one who loses when it comes to matters of God's will. Furthermore, the Holy Spirit doesn't reveal His will to only one person. He may start by telling just one person, but ultimately, He'll confirm His will to anybody who is open to hearing it.

Knowing When to Act

As you wait upon the Lord daily to receive His marching orders for you, listen especially for God's timing. Not only will the Lord show you the direction in which you are to move, but He will also reveal to you His timing and His methods. He may not give you all the details you need for the completion of a task or mission, but He will give you the information you need to take the next step in wisdom.

As you receive a directive from the Lord, look for confirmation that you have heard Him correctly. That word of confirmation may come to you as you read your Bible. It may come through a friend or perhaps in a sermon that you hear on the radio or television. It may come through a teaching that you receive at a Bible study or in a Sunday school class. Ask God to confirm to you what you have heard Him say so that you make no mistake in direction, methodology, or timing.

Many times in the Scriptures the Lord told His people to take a specific action, but then told them to wait for Him to give them the green light.

Jesus never showed up too early or too late. He always arrived right on time in keeping with what the Father was doing.

One of my favorite passages of Scripture is Psalm 62:1–2 (NKJV):

> *Truly my soul silently waits for God;*
> *From Him comes my salvation.*
> *He only is my rock and my salvation;*
> *He is my defense;*
> *I shall not be greatly moved.*

Learning to wait on God's timing is a hallmark of the mature Christian life.

Once you say to the Lord, "I'm trusting You to show me when to move," it is then the Lord's responsibility to prompt you to act. He'll plant an urgency in your heart that the time is at hand. At times the Lord has awakened me in the middle of the night with a deep impression that I was to take action the next day, or He has put such a conviction in my heart about a certain date or time that I wasn't able to escape it.

One night a number of years ago, I was on my knees in prayer when I heard God saying in my spirit, *I'm going to move you.*

I immediately asked, "When?" And before my eyes, it seemed as if a movie screen appeared, and on the screen appeared a word. It ran diagonally from the lower left-hand corner to the upper right-hand corner. In big, black letters that filled the screen I read *SEPTEMBER.*

I was stunned. It was April, and I had been in that particular pastorate less than a year. The following Monday morning, I was sitting at my desk in my study when the phone rang and a friend of mine, someone I hadn't heard from in some time, called to see if I would be interested in a position at his church. I told him I wasn't interested, but given the conversation I had just had with the Lord, I felt I needed to at least hear him out.

A few months later, I found myself moving—in September, right on time according to God's calendar.

Finding God's Will

I have met many people through the years who struggle in their desire to know God's will for their lives. My advice to them is this: do what you *think* God is calling you to do. If it isn't precisely what He desires for you to do, He'll open another door for you and move you into the precise position. From my experience, I've found that it's easier for God to position a person who is in motion and willing to move than it is for God to call a person to get up and get moving in the right direction. A man once said, "It's easier to steer a car that is started and in gear than a car that's parked."

If you are right with God and then you experience a deep restlessness, you can trust God to be at work leading you into His next lesson for you, His next place of service, His next opportunity. He will reveal to you the door that He wants you to move through.

One of my associates talked with a woman who for more than ten years felt that God was calling her to be a missionary in a foreign land. She said she had felt the call since her teenage years. As a college student, she lived overseas for a couple of years and took several student mission trips. Upon graduation, she tried repeatedly for several years to sign up with various missionary organizations. Again and again, however, she was denied the positions for which she applied. The reasons were varied—some had no openings; some stopped sending missionaries to the nations she was interested in; some were accepting only married couples; some had language requirements she hadn't fulfilled. No doors opened for her, although she still had a desire to serve God as a full-time missionary.

She finally took a job working in the United States as a social worker in the inner-city ghetto of a major metropolitan area. One day she was complaining to her pastor at the time that she couldn't understand why God had called her to be a missionary and then had slammed every door in her face.

"What door did God open for you?" her pastor asked.

She thought for a minute and said, "Well, I'm working now as a social worker with inner-city kids and their parents."

"Are you trusting God to direct your life?" the pastor asked.

"Oh, yes!" she said.

"Have you considered the possibility that the inner-city neighborhood *is* your mission field?"

She thought it over for a few moments and then said, "No, frankly, I never thought of my current job as a missionary job. I've always thought of missionaries as working overseas. I only thought of my job as a social worker as a means to pay my bills until I could join a missions organization."

Her pastor said, "I suggest that you rethink your definition of a missionary. Start to see your current work as your mission until such time as God opens another door for you."

"How will I know if another door opens?" she said.

He replied, "If God wants you to be somewhere else, He'll make that plain to you. Until then, do the work He has called you to do."

She took his advice. She later told her pastor, "My attitude changed completely toward my job. I no longer saw it as a stepping-stone to something else, but as the ministry that God had given to me. Things really began to happen. A number of families with whom I had been working began to attend church and became strong witnesses for Christ in their apartment buildings. I could see real change for the good in the lives of several teenagers and their mothers. The more I saw the projects in which I was working as a mission field, the more I was open to sharing Christ with others. The more I shared Him, the more I saw Him work to change lives. These projects *are* my mission field. I *am* doing exactly what God wants me to do!"

I don't know what God will lead you to do in your life, but I do know that He will put specific people in your path. His desire is for you to share Christ with them, perhaps by something you say, perhaps by something you do. He doesn't ask you to make things happen nearly as much as He asks that you be obedient to His leading. You can trust Him to bring the right people and circumstances to pass.

Feeling Inadequate to Fulfill God's Call

Most people have this response when they feel God calling them to undertake a specific mission or task related to the gospel: "I can't do it."

If that is your response, you're in good company. That was the response of Moses when God first called him to return to Pharaoh and demand that Pharaoh let the Israelites leave Egypt! He not only told God that he was unqualified for the job, but he asked God to find somebody else.

When God first called me to Atlanta, he gave me a vision of the city. I saw the skyline of Atlanta with dark clouds hovering over it. I knew I was in for a rough time if I went to Atlanta as a pastor, and I was right. Our first few years in Atlanta were tough ones, spiritually speaking.

God never seems to call us to tasks that are easy for us. Perhaps if they were easy, we would rely on ourselves and our gifts and abilities to accomplish the tasks. Rather, God wants us to rely solely on Him. He wants us to use our faith and to grow in our ability to trust Him fully.

The Lord always calls you to positions that have the potential to stretch you, cause you to grow, and cause you to be transformed into the person God desires for you to be. God is never content with your status quo. He wants you to continue to mature until you are exactly like Jesus Christ in your character and your responses to challenges.

If you believe God has called you to do something for Him that is too great, you're right! The job is likely to be too great for you to do in your own strength and ability. He is putting you into the same position He had the apostle Paul, who wrote, "I can do all things through Christ who strengthens me" (Phil. 4:13 NKJV).

The time to question whether you truly are doing everything that God desires for you to do is when everything seems easy and totally under your control. In all likelihood, God has something more for you to undertake for His purposes.

His Purposes, Your Refinement

The Lord's specific destiny in your life has a twofold nature:

1. It will be for the fulfillment of His purposes, not only for your individual life but also for the lives of your family members and those who are close to you and whose lives you touch. God has something for you to do that will further His kingdom on this earth.

2. It will be for your refinement. The process you face after you accept Christ as your Savior is one of refinement—of transformation, of a growing perfection. God chips away at you to smooth away the rough edges of your self-will and selfish desires. He is always about the job of bringing you to greater wholeness so that you might reflect Him more perfectly to others.

Whatever God calls you to do as a witness for Him will be for the furtherance of His work on this earth, and it will simultaneously be for the furtherance of your refinement. His destiny for you may be that of a wife and mother. Your home may be your place of ministry. The establishment of a Christian home is a great endeavor—God's desire for your home is that it be a bastion of faith, a lighthouse to others who are in spiritual danger, a haven for those who are lost and seeking God's love. Even as God uses you in building a Christian home, He will send people into your life, including your spouse and children, who will give you numerous opportunities to face certain things in your life and to come to grips with them. He will place you in relationships and situations that are opportunities for you to turn with increasing reliance upon the Lord and say, "I don't have the answer. I'm relying on You to show me what to do and say, and then to give me the courage to obey You."

Your destiny as God's witness may lie in the secular workplace. God may have a particular place of employment for you that will be your platform for sharing Christ with people who wouldn't hear about Him any other way. A Christian who is involved in the marketplace has the opportunity to witness to others on a daily basis.

I heard about a man who works as a stockbroker. He estimates that he spends an average of at least three hours a day counseling with, praying for, and encouraging people who come to his office. Some of those who come are coworkers; others are clients; some are referrals from clients or coworkers. His office is a place of active, ongoing spiritual ministry.

He said, "The more time I spend sharing Christ with others, the more time I *seem* to have to analyze the market and the greater the wisdom I seem to have in making good financial decisions for my clients. My business has grown by leaps and bounds since I told the Lord, 'My life and my career are Yours. Use me in any way You want to.' In fact, the week after I first prayed that prayer, I had the opportunity to lead three people to Christ."

This man works in an office building that is very open to the view of others. He has a glass wall with miniblinds. He said, "Not long ago, a client told me that my secretary had said to him, 'I'll buzz him as soon as his blinds open. When the blinds are closed, that means he's doing God's business. When the blinds are open, that means he's open for stockbroker business.' My client wasn't the least bit offended. He is the chairman of the board of trustees at my church. He had come to see me on church-related business, and before he left, he had also become my client. He said, 'I like the idea of having a stockbroker who does God's business.'"

Is this man in ministry? He certainly is. Is he fulfilling God's destiny for his life? Most assuredly!

A Joy in the Doing

Those who find and daily seek to fulfill God's unique destiny for sharing Christ with others experience much greater joy in life. They can hardly wait to see what God is going to do next in their lives. They are eager to get up in the mornings and to get busy.

I have this same joy in my work—every day has its own schedule, its own opportunities, its own challenges, and yes, its own problems. Even the problems, however, are exciting because I'm always on the search for how God is going to solve the problems. He comes up with the most creative solutions imaginable.

When you find your destiny in Christ, you will also find joy. Nobody will even have to talk to you about hope. You'll feel it welling up in you continually because you'll know with a certainty that

- there is still more that God wants to teach you about Himself as you read His Word.
- there is still more that God desires to show you about how to live on this earth as Christ would live.
- there is still another person with whom God desires for you to share the love of Christ and the message of the gospel.

As long as you live, God has a daily blueprint for your life that He is unfolding before you. Nobody else can fulfill what He has for you to do. And as you trust the Holy Spirit to lead you and to empower you, you can and will succeed in fulfilling His mission in your life.

God is at work in you, and He will use you to accomplish His purposes in the lives of others. At the same time, He is at work in the world around you, and He will use others to accomplish His purpose in your life. You can be assured that until your last breath, God has a purpose and a plan for your life.

Every day when I awaken I know without a doubt that

- there is more for me to learn.
- there is more for me to do.
- there is one more life for me to influence for Christ.

That gives me a new reason every day for living, and for living my life to the fullest. In that, there is hope!

I have hope because God has a blueprint for my life—a personalized plan that is still unfolding.

CHAPTER 4

GOD STILL HAS MORE FOR YOU TO BE

A man once called my associate pastor and said, "I sold my company for several million dollars last year and I'm miserable. Can you arrange an appointment for me with Dr. Stanley? I want to talk to him."

As we sat and talked he said, "I've done it all. I've succeeded in business and have all the possessions I could ever desire. I have a good wife who has stuck with me through hard times. I've been everywhere, done everything. I've sampled everything life has to offer. There's got to be more than this."

We talked for a couple of hours, and during that time, he revealed that he truly felt hopeless in his life. He saw no reason to continue to live.

He seemingly had everything, but he didn't want to live. That's a strange concept to many people, especially those who believe that happiness can be acquired with the attainment of a certain position or degree of financial security in life. In my experience as a pastor, I've found that most people assume that it's only the down-and-outers, the people who have virtually nothing and little opportunity to acquire anything, who reach the point in their lives of thinking that life is not worth living. Others assume that only those who have lost a loved one feel suicidal, or those who are deeply depressed because they are in the downward slide of an addiction. Some assume that suicide is linked solely to those who have terrible haunting secrets or who suffer from intense physical pain or severe illness.

The fact is, many wealthy and successful people have been in precisely the position this man was in. They have tasted the very best of what they believe life has to offer, yet they ask, "Is that all there is?"

I heard about a young woman who several decades ago had been a well-known athlete in state and regional circles. She had won the top competitions in her chosen sport. At the pinnacle of her success, she married a successful young businessman, and they had a beautiful daughter. Within a year or so after the birth of their daughter, the young woman awoke one morning and said to herself, Is this all there is? She concluded that even though she was not yet thirty years old, life was over for her. There were no more of what she called "glory moments" left ahead.

She turned to various types of prescription medications to nurse her disappointment with life and soon was addicted to them. She ended up in a mental hospital, where she was treated for several weeks for severe clinical depression. Not yet thirty—with everything to live for—but she found life not worth living.

Another woman who was counseled by a friend of mine spent several years in what she called a "search for meaning." At age nineteen, she had married a physician who was ten years older than she was. Within the next decade, they had four children—a son and three daughters. She and her husband were invited to all the prominent social events in their community, and she participated casually in several of the "right" clubs and volunteer organizations, but only for social reasons. She lived in a beautiful home, enrolled her children in an exclusive private school, and then embarked on her own private spiritual odyssey. For eight years she dabbled in several Eastern religious cults. She read dozens of books and manuals that taught her how to engage in various spiritual practices—none of which filled the growing void she felt in her life.

The more she read, the more depressed she became. The more she sought meaning for her life, the less meaning she found. She began to see a psychiatrist, but found that most of what her therapist said to her was meaningless and unproductive. She withdrew from her social group, then her family. Finally, she ended up in a psychiatric hospital where she was given shock treatments. Upon her release, her mother recommended that she begin to see my friend, a Christian counselor.

Both women had it all in the eyes of the world: success, money, family, social standing, possessions, education, accomplishments, a certain degree of notoriety. And they found deep, inner satisfaction in none of it.

God Desires to Do an "Inside" Job

I asked the man who came to see me if he had ever accepted the Lord Jesus into his life. He told me that he believed he was a Christian since he had been baptized in one of the mainline denominations as an infant. I asked him who Christ was in his life today.

He said, "I'm not sure. A business associate recommended that I come to your church, and frankly, I've never heard anybody preach like you preach. I've heard things I've never heard before. That's one of the reasons I came to see you."

I asked him, "Do you want to be *sure* that Christ is in your life? Do you want to know with certainty that you are forgiven?" He said, "Yes." And so I led him in a sinner's prayer.

Afterward, I said, "Now, no matter how you feel right this moment, the Bible tells us that you have believed and received Christ into your life. He is present with you, and He will never leave you." I opened my Bible and had him read this passage of Scripture aloud:

> *If you confess with your mouth the Lord Jesus and believe in your heart that God has raised Him from the dead, you will be saved. For with the heart one believes unto righteousness, and with the mouth confession is made unto salvation. For the Scripture says, "Whoever believes on Him will not be put to shame."... For "whoever calls on the name of the LORD shall be saved."* (Rom. 10:9–11, 13 NKJV)

"Do you believe that God raised Christ from the dead?" I asked him.

"I do," he said.

"And do you believe that Jesus Christ is in your life right now?"

"I do," he said.

"Then you *are* in right standing with God," I said. "You have been forgiven of all your sins."

Then I turned to these verses and asked him to read them aloud: "For He Himself has said, 'I will never leave you nor forsake you.' So we may boldly say: 'The LORD is my helper; I will not fear'" (Heb. 13:5–6 NKJV).

I pointed to another verse from the same passage in Hebrews where he had been reading aloud: "Jesus Christ is the same yesterday, today, and forever" (Heb. 13:8 NKJV).

"Do you believe the Lord is with you not only right now, but always?" I asked him. "Do you believe that the Lord is never going to change, never going to leave you?"

He replied, "On the basis of what you just had me read, I do believe that."

"We know with certainty that we have Christ with us always because Jesus said that He would send His Holy Spirit to those who believed," I said, "and that the Holy Spirit would *seal* the presence of Christ in our lives. That's a seal that can never be broken—not by any person or any situation or circumstance."

And again I turned to Scripture so he could read God's truth for himself: "Having believed, you were sealed with the Holy Spirit of promise, who is the guarantee of our inheritance until the redemption of the purchased possession, to the praise of His glory" (Eph. 1:13–14 NKJV).

"The Holy Spirit is Christ's own Spirit within you," I said. "Do you believe you have the Holy Spirit at work in your life?"

"If that's what the Bible says, then that's what I'm going to believe," he said.

"Then everything that Jesus *is*—all of His attributes and His power—*is* available to you at all times. The Holy Spirit is with you fully, not just partially. He gives you *all* of Himself, not just some of Himself," I said. "You may not feel as if you have all of Christ's own Spirit at work in you right now, but feelings are just that—feelings. Emotions rise and fall. Emotions come and go. But God's Word is true. You can count on it."

"I do feel really clean right now," he said. "I feel as if the entire slate of my past has been wiped clean. Is it right for me to feel that way?"

"It sure is!" I encouraged him. "That feeling is typical for those who receive Christ into their lives. That's a feeling many people have when they realize they have been forgiven and restored to a right relationship with God. But even if you don't always have the feelings that you have right now, the fact remains that Christ is in your life. That's the main point I want you to see. You have Christ in you, now and always. His presence doesn't ride the waves of your feelings. His presence *abides*. It's firmly rooted, and nothing can destroy His presence in you. You have established an eternal relationship with God, your heavenly Father."

Then I added, "From here on—from this moment until the last moment of your life—God is primarily going to do an *inside job* in your life. What you end up doing with your life on the outside—in your investments, your family, the church, the community—all of that will flow from whatever you allow God to do inside you first."

God's Purpose Is for You to Be Fruitful

The man still had questions. He saw the future as a great unknown, in his terms, "a big gray without anything moving in it."

I said to him, "God understands where you are at. Jesus has felt what you are feeling."

"How could He feel what I've been feeling?" he said with a note of incredulity. "He was God's Son. He wasn't a successful businessman who faced retirement without a challenge."

"No," I said, "but the Bible tells us that Jesus felt every emotion known to humankind. Hebrews 4:15 [NKJV] says, 'We do not have a High Priest who cannot sympathize with our weaknesses, but was in all points tempted as we are, yet without sin.' Jesus felt emotionally everything that you are feeling—wondering if His purpose in life was over, if He had done everything He was destined to do. That was part of His great agony in the Garden of Gethsemane just before His crucifixion."

"Yes," he said ruefully, "but the answer for Him was death, wasn't it? His life *was* over."

"No, not at all," I said. "The Cross was not the end of Christ's life. In many ways, it was just the beginning of it. God's answer to Jesus was not that His ministry was over, but that only one phase of His ministry was completed. The most important part of His ministry still lay ahead. It involved the Cross, the Resurrection, and the greater ministry of Christ through the sending of the Holy Spirit."

He said to me in terms that a businessman might use, "His job description just changed . . . is that what you are telling me?"

"His job description got larger," I said. "There was more that God the Father intended for His Son to be and do. Up to that point, Jesus was most assuredly God's Son. He was completely filled with the Holy Spirit. He bore all the marks of divinity in His Spirit. He certainly had taught the people about how to be in right relationship with God, and His miracles had shown the people that God was a loving, healing, reconciling heavenly Father. But at the point when Jesus was in the Garden of Gethsemane, Jesus was not yet the Savior of the world, the one complete and definitive sacrifice for the salvation of the human heart. He was not yet the risen Lord. He had not yet ascended to heaven where He was to be seated as our great High Priest at the right hand of God the Father. He was not yet our Mediator and Advocate. He had not yet sent the Holy Spirit to empower and to give daily counsel to His church."

"Are you telling me that there's more that God has for me to do?"

"Absolutely," I said. "There's not only more for you to do, but also more for you to *be*."

"What is it that God still wants me to be?" he asked.

"He wants you to bear the fruit of the Holy Spirit—all of the hallmarks of the Spirit's presence," I said. "He wants you to be His love in action."

And friend, regardless of your situation today, God desires for you to *be* that too. He desires for you to bear the fruit of His Spirit and to be a force of His love in the world.

Galatians 5:22–23 (NKJV) lists the qualities of fruit associated with the Holy Spirit: "But the fruit of the Spirit is love, joy, peace, long-suffering, kindness, goodness, faithfulness, gentleness, self-control."

Love. The fruit of the Holy Spirit is first and foremost love: "The love of God has been poured out in our hearts by the Holy Spirit who was given to us" (Rom. 5:5 NKJV). All of the other qualities associated with having the Holy Spirit flow from the presence of God's love in you.

Joy is love enjoying all of the goodness of God and all of the wonders of His creation.

Peace is love resting on the promises of God and expecting the fulfillment of the promises in your life.

Longsuffering, or patience, is love waiting for God to reveal to you and in you what He desires to reveal.

Kindness is love reacting to those around you.

Goodness is love choosing to do what is right and good in God's eyes.

Faithfulness is love keeping its worth—remaining true to its Source and clinging to its foundation in Christ Jesus.

Gentleness is love empathizing with people in need or pain.

Self-control is love actively resisting temptation.

As you open yourself to embracing, and then manifesting, the fullness of God's love in you, these other qualities of character are going to emerge in your life. You don't have to work up your joy or peace. You don't have to strive to become patient, kind, or gentle. You don't have to say to yourself in the mirror each morning, "I'm going to have self-control. I'm going to be faithful." All you do is say to your heavenly Father with a sincere and humble heart, "I receive Your love. I believe You love me, and I accept with an open heart the love You have for me."

Countless books on the market tell you how to be a positive, upbeat person. Most of these books give you techniques for becoming happy—saying certain things to yourself repeatedly, meditating on happy memories, or imaging yourself in pleasant environments. The emphasis is nearly always, however, on things you are supposed to *do*. These books tell you how to rev up your generator so that happy, contented feelings are created by you, in you, and then through you to others.

Although some of these techniques can be helpful for relieving stress, the genuine joy, peace, and contentment that you desire in life are not feelings you can generate on your own. They are solely the work of the Holy Spirit in you. These qualities of human character are developed and manifested in your life only as you receive, by faith, the love of God.

God's purpose in you from the moment you accept Jesus Christ as your Savior, until the moment that you die and enter His presence to live with Him forever, is this: to produce in you the qualities that were and are in Christ Jesus. He desires to transform you into the very likeness of His Son. That's what the apostle Paul referred to when he wrote that we are to grow in Christ until

> *we all come to the unity of the faith and of the knowledge of the Son of God, to a perfect man, to the measure of the stature of the fullness of Christ; that we should no longer be children, tossed to and fro and carried about with every wind of doctrine, by the trickery of men, in the cunning craftiness of deceitful plotting, but, speaking the truth in love, may grow up in all things into Him who is the head—Christ.* (Eph. 4:13–15 NKJV)

As you grow in Christ, you not only manifest His character qualities in your life, but you are equipped and empowered to do certain things.

First, the Holy Spirit equips you to know how to express God's love.

When you choose to receive God's love—and to experience it daily, walk in it, and let it fill your heart—then God's love becomes the guiding and ruling force of your life. Anytime you are faced with a decision or choice, your immediate response deep within your spirit is this: What would my loving heavenly Father do?

Note, however, that this is never your own human love. It is *agape* love, God's love. God's love is always just, even as it is merciful. God's love is always based upon God's absolutes. God's love doesn't deny sin; it seeks to remove sin. God's love doesn't gloss over evil; it seeks to eradicate evil and replace it with God's goodness.

Some Christian bookstores sell a little fabric bracelet. Woven into the bracelet are these four initials: *WWJD*. The letters stand for "What Would Jesus Do?" They serve as a reminder that your response to virtually every situation or circumstance you face should reflect what your loving Savior would do. You are to be God's love in action.

God's Holy Spirit in you will always reveal what God desires for you to do. The Holy Spirit always answers your question, What would my loving heavenly Father do in this situation? The very purpose of the Holy Spirit is to reveal God's wisdom and to help you manifest God's character. The Holy Spirit does this in a very practical way by bringing to your remembrance what the Word of God says. Jesus taught, "The Helper, the Holy Spirit, whom the Father will send in My name, He will teach you all things, and bring to your remembrance all things that I said to you" (John 14:26 NKJV).

The Holy Spirit also works through your conscience. If you genuinely want to know what God desires you to do to show His love to other people or to manifest His love in specific settings, He will make known God's desire in your life. He'll work through your conscience to reveal to you what is right and what is wrong.

I recently read about an experience of a man who was speaking to a group of college students. He was giving a lecture on morality and ethics, and the students were raising objections to his claim that sex outside marriage was wrong. He gave numerous examples and statistics showing the benefits of keeping sexual relations within the marriage covenant. He also quoted well-respected and famous people who had addressed this issue through the centuries. A number of the students, however, balked at his conclusions and argued with him about the benefits of free sex and living together in a sexual relationship without the constraints of legal, religious, or societal laws.

He finally said to them, "I want you to close your eyes and get calm for a minute. Cool off. Let your mind stop racing." He waited for the students to comply. Then he said, "Now I want you to listen to your heart for a minute. Don't reason this issue with your mind. Listen to what your heart tells you."

He waited a full five minutes in silence. Then he asked the students, "What did your hearts say?"

Almost to the student, those who had disagreed so vigorously with him admitted, "I may have to rethink this. I may have been too hasty in my arguments." One student said, "I thought I really believed what I was saying to you, but I don't think I really do. Deep inside I believe that sex outside marriage is wrong."

God can and will speak to your conscience if you allow Him to do so. The Holy Spirit within you will always nudge you toward God's commandments and His goodness. He will always move you toward God's love and toward what is right in God's eyes. God's Word declares that the work of the Holy Spirit is to "direct your [heart] into the love of God and into the patience of Christ" (2 Thess. 3:5 NKJV). He will not lead you to do what is wrong; rather, He will lead you to what is absolutely, clearly, and definitively right—not only for you in the moment, but for you and all other believers in Christ Jesus for all eternity.

Second, the Holy Spirit equips you to manifest love in very practical ways.

The Love Chapter in the Bible is considered to be 1 Corinthians 13. This is not a passage about the theory of God's love. It is a very practical chapter. Love is not about speaking eloquent words, writing lyrical poems, or having faith in God or a knowledge of the Bible.

Love is not even about doing good works—such as feeding the poor or dying a martyr's death—just for the sake of doing good works.

Love is about the way in which you work and give witness to your faith. You can witness to a person about your religion—even your faith in Christ—in a way that isn't pleasing to the Holy Spirit. You can do good works—even good works associated with your church—and see absolutely no consequence from them for the kingdom of God. Love is to be your very motivation for doing and saying what you do and say.

Let's take a look at very specific points Paul made in 1 Corinthians 13:

- "Love suffers long and is kind" (v. 4 NKJV). Love manifests itself in patience and kindness, regardless of what you are engaged in doing or in what relationship you may be struggling.
- "Love does not envy; love does not parade itself, is not puffed up; does not behave rudely, does not seek its own" (vv. 4–5 NKJV). Love doesn't desire another person's spouse or possessions. Love isn't showy. It doesn't call attention to itself. It doesn't deal harshly or bypass manners and courtesy. Love works in hidden, secret ways; its best work is behind the scenes. It wants only what is good for another person.
- Love "is not provoked, thinks no evil; does not rejoice in iniquity, but rejoices in the truth" (vv. 5–6 NKJV). Love doesn't allow itself to be enticed into anything contrary to God's laws. If someone says to you, "If you love me, you'll lie for me," or "If you love me, you'll prove it by having sex with me even though we aren't married," or "If you love me, you'll commit an illegal act for me so I can get out of a jam I'm in," the person is not asking you to show love. The person is asking you to join in sin. Genuine *agape* love doesn't engage in sin, regardless of how much you want to help another person.
- Love "bears all things, believes all things, hopes all things, endures all things" (v. 7 NKJV). God's *agape* love working in you and through you lasts. It never gives up on another person's potential in Christ Jesus. It always believes that a person can be redeemed. It always believes that God's promises are true and that they will come to pass. It doesn't waver in times of persecution, rejection, or assault.

- "Love never fails" (v. 8 NKJV). Love is never the wrong response to make. Your knowledge is always limited. Even your human understanding of God's Word is sometimes incomplete or in error because you have a finite mind and you will never understand fully all that God has revealed in His Word. But love is not limited. You always have the capacity to show love, even if you can't quote a particular verse of Scripture to back up your position. You can always show love even if you don't have a logical reason or argument to explain why you love as you do.

A life without love flowing through it—love that comes from God and is shown to others—is a life without meaning. It is an empty existence.

But a life in which love is being manifested in practical ways to others is a life with meaning and purpose. It is a life worth living!

You Are God's Work in Progress

The Holy Spirit is at work in you to create the likeness of Christ in you and to reveal to you God's will for your life and God's response to your circumstances.

You are a work in progress. God is molding and fashioning you into a person with whom He wants to live forever.

Because of this, you have the hope that you are not going to be the same person tomorrow that you are today. If you are opening your life to God's love, and you desire to have God's love work in you and through you, then you are going to be more like Christ tomorrow than you are right now. Next week, you will be even more like Christ. Next year, you will be even more like Him. And so on. There is always more for you to *be*. There is always more inner work that the Holy Spirit desires to do.

Jesus is the "author and finisher" of your faith (Heb. 12:2 NKJV). He is writing His story into your life. He is in the process of replicating His character in you. And the good news is this: "He who has begun a good work in you will complete it until the day of Jesus Christ" (Phil. 1:6 NKJV).

Anything that God does in your life will last. It will be for your perfection, your wholeness. And it will endure throughout all the ages. What Christ is doing in you, day by day, week in and week out, year in and year out, is a good work that has eternal value. You are not only a work in progress, but you are a good work in progress. God is building into you the qualities of Himself that will last forever.

Paul wrote this encouragement that God will see His work through to completion: "May the God of peace Himself sanctify you completely; and may your whole spirit, soul, and body be preserved blameless at the coming of our Lord Jesus Christ. He who calls you is faithful, who also will do it" (1 Thess. 5:23–24 NKJV).

Friend, the fact that God is relentlessly and lovingly at work in you, transforming you into the very likeness of His Son, Jesus Christ, is a powerful reason to have hope! You may not like who you are today. But God is at work changing you into a person you are going to love. You may not like your life today. But God is at work transforming you and preparing you for a life you are going to love.

You may think there is no reason to live. But until the day you are taken home to be with the Lord, you have every reason to live— God hasn't yet finished His work in you. There is more He wants to do inside you and then through you.

The Lord is utterly committed to this transformation of your life. I trust you will join me today in making this statement of hope:

I have hope because God is at work in me, and the work that He is doing is a good work with eternal benefit!

CHAPTER 5

GOD STILL HAS MORE TO SAY TO YOU

When was the last time you heard God speak to you in your spirit?

I believe God desires to communicate with each of us on a daily basis—in fact, as often as we need to hear from Him, which may be several times in a day. He always has a message for us that is more timely than the daily news and more important than the message that any person on earth can give.

Not long ago a woman told me that her mother-in-law had died a few weeks earlier after a very painful experience with stomach cancer. I began to offer my sympathy when the woman interrupted me and said, "I'm glad this happened."

I was a bit taken aback. "You are?" I asked.

"Oh, yes," she said. "This wasn't a negative thing at all. It was the most positive experience in her life and certainly one of the most positive experiences in mine."

Most people would consider stomach cancer to be anything but positive. I was interested in hearing more of her story, which she was happy to tell.

"My mother-in-law was one of the most bitter, spiteful, difficult women I have ever met. I knew from the first minute she laid eyes on me that she was determined to be my enemy," she began. "In fact, my husband and I eloped so we wouldn't have to deal with her at our wedding ceremony. During the fifteen years that I knew her before her diagnosis with cancer, I never heard a kind word from her lips—except to our daughter. She had a soft spot in her heart for our daughter, but not for anyone else. She wasn't mean only to me, but to my husband, to her other two sons, and to everyone she encountered. Repairmen told me that they dreaded a call from her home, and even the kindest clergyman we know had a difficult time with her rebukes and sarcasm."

"She must have been a woman with a great deal of inner pain," I said.

"Yes," she replied. "I didn't realize how much inner pain she had, however, until after her diagnosis. Up to that time, I just figured she was a hateful, mean woman. I didn't take the time or make the effort to see beyond her facade."

"She may not have let you see inside her," I said.

"I believe that's right," she agreed. "She had a stone wall around her heart. And she kept this stone wall in place for several weeks after her doctor told her she had cancer. Initially, she was given only a few weeks to live. It was amazing to everyone who knew her and knew her condition that she lived nearly five months."

"And you believe that was the grace of God?" I asked.

"Yes," she said. "What happened was this. She refused all offers of help except those from my husband and me. We were the only ones she would allow to enter her home to fix meals for her and to change her bed and do her laundry. When the pain was intense, she'd ask us to read to her or to stay and converse with her to help take her mind off the pain. As the days went by and she saw that I was caring for her with love and concern—not with criticism or hate—she began to tell me her story. I began to understand why she was filled with such anger."

"Was it something from her childhood?" I guessed.

"Actually from her teen years," she said. "A woman in her church accused her of stealing funds that the youth group had collected for a ski trip. The accusations were made in a very hurtful and public way, and my mother-in-law was given little chance to defend herself or to reply to the charges. She hadn't taken the money, but ironically, about the same time she had found twenty dollars in a small coin purse in the gutter of a street near her home. She had spent the money, figuring that she was the benefactor of finders, keepers. When she offered this explanation as the reason she had had more spending money of late, the woman refused to believe her story and not only called her a thief but a liar.

"My mother-in-law became so angry that she dropped out of church and turned her back on God. For years she had told me she was an atheist. After her diagnosis she modified that to say she didn't believe in God because if there was a God, He should be just and righteous, and there had been no justice on her behalf in this unfortunate situation."

"So she had been angry and bitter for decades," I said.

"Yes, for forty-nine years. The more she suffered with her disease, the more she concluded that there was no God of mercy or kindness. She couldn't explain away, however, the peace that my husband, daughter, and I felt in our hearts—or the kindness and love that we showered upon her. Bit by bit, she began to soften. She even started asking us to read some of the Psalms to her when she was in pain. We had a couple of conversations about heaven too."

"Did she accept the Lord as her Savior before she died?" I asked.

"Yes, but it happened in a way that I would never have anticipated," she said as tears welled up in her eyes.

"One day when I went over to fix dinner for her, our daughter went along. She said, 'Granny Lou, I love you. And Jesus told me to tell you that He loves you too.' I froze in my tracks. I steeled myself for what I felt sure would be my mother-in-law's reply, probably something like, 'That's nice for you to believe.' Instead, she said, 'I know He does, dear. He told me so Himself last night.'

"She looked up and I'm sure she read my face, which no doubt expressed great surprise and pleasure. She said, 'I saw Jesus last night. He came to the foot of my bed in a pool of bright light and said, "Lou, I'm here to tell you that I love you. I want you to come live with Me."'"

"Wonderful!" I said.

She continued, "I was so stunned, all I could stammer was, 'That's great, Mother Lou.' She said, 'I know you probably think it's strange He would come calling on me like that, and I was pretty surprised myself. I asked Him, "How could you love an old hag like me?" He said, "You won't be an old hag when you are living with Me." And then He was gone.'

"Not long after that, she asked my husband to pray the sinner's prayer with her. And about a week later, she died. Just before she died, she said, 'I wasted a lot of years railing against God. Instead of my doing all the talking against Him, I should have done a little more listening to Him.'"

"What a tremendous testimony!" I said.

"My mother-in-law isn't the only one with a testimony," she said. "The Lord did a great thing in my own heart through this. I discovered in caring for my mother-in-law that I had failed to love as Christ loved. I repented of the hatred I had held toward my mother-in-law and asked God to forgive me and to help me love her as He loved her. He softened my heart and gave me compassion and tenderness toward her that I would never have believed were possible. I find myself looking at difficult people with new eyes. In fact, I'm considering taking a volunteer position with the hospice program. I believe the Lord still has things to teach me and ways to use me."

"I feel certain that He does," I said.

"One thing I know with certainty," she said as our conversation drew to a close, "God can cross *any* barriers we might put up.

I'm grateful that He still had something to say to my mother-in-law. I have a new faith that He still has something to say to me too."

Yes, a thousand times yes. God does still have something to say to each one of us. He never reaches the place where He doesn't have a message that is precisely for us.

God Desires to Communicate with You

When we think of communicating with God, very often we think about our talking to God. In conversing with people through the years about prayer, I've discovered that most people spend about 99 percent of their time talking to God—telling Him what they want Him to do, asking Him for things they want Him to give them, voicing their belief in His promises, even pleading with Him at times to do things in their lives that He has already done!

I've met people who have asked God on numerous occasions to save their souls. One young woman said, "I've been saved three times." And she could recount each occasion in vivid detail. She had "walked the aisle" at her church when she was a young teenager in response to a salvation altar call, then had given her life to Christ when she was a teenager attending a youth camp, and finally, had prayed to ask the Lord to come into her life during a prayer meeting in her college dorm room. A friend of mine asked her, "Which time worked?"

The young woman replied, "Each time I felt God forgiving me of my sins."

The fact was, God forgave her sinful nature and entered her life the first time she asked Him to do so. She was converted to Christ the first time she turned to God to receive His forgiveness.

The fact also is, God forgives you each time you come to Him and confess that you have sinned. He forgives you and then assists you in repenting of your sins.

Your salvation is a definitive work in your life the moment you accept that Jesus died on the cross for your sins. His indwelling Holy Spirit continues to convict you of areas that need changing in your life—habits that need to be dropped or acquired; attitudes that need to be altered; automatic responses that need to be transformed to line up with God's Word and the life of Christ. You don't need to plead with God to save you or to forgive you or to change you. He responds to you the moment you turn to Him to receive His love. And He then begins a renewal work that is ongoing in you the rest of your life.

People who repeatedly ask God to forgive them and to save their souls need to accept the certain fact that He has. They then need to forgive themselves and move forward in their lives.

Other people repeatedly ask God for things with an attitude of worry. They want to make sure God doesn't forget them. They aren't 100 percent certain that God is going to provide what they need. They spend most of their days struggling and striving to make sure they have not only enough material substance, but an abundance of material wealth. And then, they add a prayer, "Oh, God, please give me this, please give me that."

Jesus taught His disciples to pray, "Our Father in heaven . . . give us this day our daily bread" (Matt. 6:9, 11 NKJV). The concept of daily bread goes far beyond a loaf of whole wheat bread for physical nourishment. *Bread* is a term that refers to everything that is necessary for wholeness in life. It refers to the things we need physically, but also to the things we need mentally, emotionally, and spiritually. Jesus told His disciples on one occasion, "I have food [bread] to eat of which you do not know." When His disciples asked for an explanation, He said, "My food is to do the will of Him who sent Me, and to finish His work" (John 4:32–34 NKJV).

When you ask the Lord to give you your daily bread, you are also to mean, "Give me today what You know I need to carry out Your purposes for me on the earth. I trust You to meet all my needs."

Now you are to pray specifically for the Lord to defeat evil whenever and wherever you encounter it—in yourself or in others. That is the foremost role of petitioning the Lord in prayer. In Jericho, Jesus asked a man who was blind, "What do you want Me to do for you?" The man was obviously blind; nevertheless Jesus asked. You are to tell the Lord specifically what you want Him to do to reverse evil, destroy evil, and defeat the enemy in your life. (See Mark 10:51.)

About your daily needs, however, you are not to worry. Jesus taught,

> *Do not worry about your life, what you will eat or what you will drink; nor about your body, what you will put on. Is not life more than food and the body more than clothing? Look at the birds of the air, for they neither sow nor reap nor gather into barns; yet your heavenly Father feeds them. Are you not of more value than they? Which of you by worrying can add one cubit to his stature? . . . For after all these things the Gentiles seek. For your heavenly Father knows that you need all these things. But seek first the kingdom of God and His righteousness, and all these things shall be added to you.* (Matt. 6:25–27, 32–33 NKJV)

Your communication with God is also to include praise and thanksgiving. You are to

> *enter into His gates with thanksgiving,*
> *And into His courts with praise.*
> *Be thankful to Him, and bless His name.*
> *For the* LORD *is good;*
> *His mercy is everlasting,*
> *And His truth endures to all generations.* (Ps. 100:4–5 NKJV)

Great is the Lord, and greatly to be praised!

"With thanksgiving, let your requests be made known to God," Paul advised the Philippians (4:6 NKJV). You make your petitions with thanksgiving, fully expecting God to hear you and answer you *according to the will of heaven*.

But in all of your praise and thanksgiving and voicing of requests, you must take time to listen. God desires to say something to you.

Two-Way Communication

Think about your relationship with someone you love. If you do all the talking in that relationship, it isn't truly a relationship, is it? True communication is a two-way street. You express yourself, and then you listen to the other person. He or she expresses something to you, and you respond. In that way, decisions are reached, consensus is built, agreements are forged, problems are resolved, secrets are shared, dreams and ideas are revealed, information is exchanged, attitudes are influenced, encouragement is offered, advice is given and received, and a sense of intimacy is developed.

If you spend all of your time telling God about your problems and needs, your feelings, your hopelessness, your desires, you are missing out on hearing about God's desires, His feelings, and His dreams for your life and for the lives of others. You also will miss out on hearing about how God feels about you.

Do You *Want* to Hear from God?

Dr. Stanley," a man admitted to me, "I'm not sure I *want* to know how God feels about me." If that's your attitude, you likely are carrying a load of guilt.

Define and examine closely what you think God would be displeased about, ask Him to forgive you of that habit or past deed, and then go on in your life with a determination never to do that thing again. The feeling you have of condemnation is *not* God's feeling toward you. It is your response toward your disobedience of His commandments. The apostle Paul very clearly taught that the purpose of the Law is to bring you to just this point of conviction of sin. When you line up your life against God's absolutes and His lasting commandments, you fall short. You know you have erred.

Anytime that you attempt to compare yourself and your achievements to God, you also fall short. Consider Romans 3:23 (NKJV): "For all have sinned and fall short of the glory of God." When you stand before the absolute perfection of God, you must admit your weaknesses, your failures, your inabilities, your shortcomings.

God does not change His nature in order to make you feel better about yourself. That is something human beings often try to do—alter their behavior so that other people will respond to them in ways that are warm and accepting. God does not change. Rather, God holds out to you His great love and His ideal for you—that you can be transformed by the power of His Holy Spirit working in you, so that you are enabled to do His will and walk in His ways. God's desire is *not* that you feel condemned or guilty, but that anytime you have these feelings, you turn to Him immediately to receive His forgiveness and experience His love.

God always feels love and forgiveness toward you, regardless of what you have done or how much you may have rejected Him in the past.

As a young minister drove me to the airport, we had an opportunity to talk. He told me that he still struggled in his perception of God. He said, "I've heard people whom I admire greatly tell me that God is a loving God—including you, Dr. Stanley—but I still have a picture of God as a stern judge. I guess I grew up thinking, *There's God, way up there, sitting in His judgment seat just waiting for me to do something so He can whack me*. It's hard for me to think of God as being very close or very touchable."

I said, "Tell me about your father."

As you might imagine, his father had been a very tough disciplinarian. "My father was hardly ever there," he said. "He traveled a lot in his work, and when he was home, Mom made sure that he punished us for things we had done while he was away. Dad had very strict rules, and he expected us to follow them even when he was gone."

"If that was the case," I said, "I'll guess that you dreaded your father's coming home."

"Yes," he said, "I suppose I did."

"But at the same time you wanted his approval?" I guessed.

"Oh, yes," he said. "I thought my father was everything. I very much wanted my father's approval, but he was hardly ever there to see me do anything that he could approve. I think he made it to only one of my basketball games, and as I recall, I was so nervous that he was there that I didn't do very well that night."

"Have you given God all of the traits that you experienced in your earthly father?" I asked. "Have you made God just a bigger version of your dad?"

He thought for a minute and then said, "Yes, I think that's what I've done."

Since our time was short, I encouraged him to go back to his Bible and read about Jesus in Matthew, Mark, Luke, and John. "Jesus told His disciples, 'If you had known Me, you would have known My Father also. . . . The words that I speak to you I do not speak on My own authority; but the Father who dwells in Me does the works. Believe Me that I am in the Father and the Father in Me' [John 14:7, 10–11 NKJV]. When we see Jesus, we are seeing the very nature and character of the Father at work."

I continued, "Get a clear picture of Jesus. With your spiritual eyes, see Jesus as He gently touched those who were sick. See Him as He picked up little children and held them and blessed them, even when other people clamored for His attention. See Jesus as He stopped to talk to people along the way. He always had time for people. He healed all who came to Him. He had close fellowship with people who were called sinners by the religious society."

As I talked about Jesus, I could see tears form in this man's eyes. "Get a clear picture of Jesus on the cross. He died so that others might come to know the Father as intimately as He knew Him—so that they might be one with each other and one with the Father. When you get a really vivid picture of Jesus, you'll have the right picture of God."

He nodded. I continued, "Would the Jesus that you know from the Gospels sit on a big throne high and far away from you, judging you harshly every time you made a mistake?"

"No," he said very softly. "He wouldn't."

"Then neither does God the Father," I said.

When you see God as standing in harsh judgment of you, you are projecting onto Him your feelings of guilt, judgment, and condemnation. You may very well be projecting onto God the failures and faults of your earthly father. Own up to your feelings, and ask God to help you get a true picture of who He is and what He is like. I believe He will reveal Himself to you. Own up to your failures and sins, and ask Him to forgive you and to help you change your ways. *He will!*

God's Message of Love for You

I believe there are at least three messages that God desires to communicate to each one of us on a daily basis.

The first message God wants to convey to us is this: "I love you." We may know that in a broad, general sense. Most of us would readily agree with the childhood chorus, "Jesus loves me, this I know." But on an ongoing daily basis, God has a unique way of expressing His love for us. We must have keen spiritual ears to hear this message.

A woman told a marriage counselor, "My husband never tells me he loves me."

The marriage counselor turned and asked the husband, "Is that true?"

The man replied very contritely, "I guess it is."

The counselor asked, "Do you love your wife?"

"I do," the man said. "I love her a lot."

"Are you afraid to tell her that you love her?" the counselor asked.

"No," the man said, "I'm not scared to tell her I love her."

The counselor asked, "Then do you know why you never tell her that you love her?"

He thought for a moment and said simply, "Well, I think the main reason is, she never stops talking long enough for me to say so."

Is it possible that the main reason you have never heard God tell you how much He loves you is that you have never stopped petitioning Him long enough to listen to His voice?

God desires to communicate His great love for you on a daily basis. He desires to tell you how much you mean to Him and how He delights in having a relationship with you.

I once talked to a young woman who was very much in love with the man who eventually became her husband. She said, "He does the nicest things to tell me he loves me."

"Like what?" I asked her.

"Oh, he leaves me little notes here and there. He might put a fresh rose in my mailbox or leave a loving message on my answering machine. Every day it's something different." Then she added, "I hope he never runs out of ideas!"

God never runs out of ideas about how to tell you in unique ways that He loves you. His love may come to you in the form of an unexpected blessing, a call from someone you haven't heard from in a while, a kindness extended to you by a total stranger, the opportunity to hear a favorite song, a hug from a child. Each day God has a new way of sending His love message to you.

God wants you to know several things about His love.

God wants to tell you that His love is a gift.

God wants you to know that His love for you is a "perfect gift" (James 1:17 NKJV). There is nothing that you can do to deserve this gift or to deserve a greater expression of this gift. His love for you has always been, is now, and always will be an infinite love.

The only thing you can do in conjunction with His gift is to receive it and to thank Him for it. There is no earning His perfect gift; there is no exchanging it.

There was a situation in my life in which I told God precisely what I wanted Him to do to a particular person. I was hurt, frustrated, and impatient. I trusted God to be my avenger, but I wanted Him to do His avenging right away! He responded to me by speaking in my heart, *I can't do that.*

"Why not?" I asked.

Because My love for that person is as perfect as My love for you. If I didn't love that person as much as I love you, you couldn't trust My love. You couldn't count on My love always being there for you when you sin. You couldn't count on My love being there for you when you hurt others. But because I love this person as much as I love you, you can count on My love.

I learned through that experience that we can always trust a perfect love. Such love comes from God alone. He is the giver of this kind of love to each one of us.

God wants to assure you that His love is everlasting.

Moods change. Emotions fluctuate from day to day, sometimes from hour to hour. God's love for you has no variation. You have this word from the Lord: "I have loved you with an everlasting love" (Jer. 31:3 NKJV).

Paul described God's everlasting love in this way:

> *For I am persuaded that neither death nor life, nor angels nor principalities nor powers, nor things present nor things to come, nor height nor depth, nor any other created thing, shall be able to separate us from the love of God which is in Christ Jesus our Lord.* (Rom. 8:38–39 NKJV)

You can't start God's love flowing toward you because it already is flowing toward you. You can't deter it, stop it, interrupt it, or change it. His banner over you is love, and it is always love. You didn't deserve it, and therefore, you can't do anything to "undeserve" it.

God's love toward you has nothing to do with *your* nature. It has everything to do with *His* nature.

God wants to tell you that His sacrificial love is available to all.

God sent His only Son, Jesus Christ, to die as an expression of how much God loves us. God sacrificed His beloved Son on our behalf—on my behalf, on your behalf, on behalf of every person alive today. There is no higher price that could ever have been paid.

On a daily basis, God will bring people across your path whom you may find to be troublesome, irksome, or a nuisance. He does so as a constant reminder to you, "I love even him. I love even her." You continually are called to face the fact that you are more like those whom you dislike than you are willing to admit. You have flaws and failures and quirks that annoy or anger others. Only when you accept the fact that Christ died for you, *and* Christ died for every other person you encounter, can you begin to love others as Christ loves them.

A number of years ago, several of my friends told me how a particular man had ridiculed me. He had made it very public that he didn't like me or what I stood for. I categorized him as a braggart and a bully and pretty much wrote him off as someone I'd try to avoid if at all possible. In plain language, I decided that I didn't like him. Never mind that I didn't know him very well. I concluded that if even a small fraction of what I had been told he had said and done was true, then I didn't like him.

Some time later we were both on the same program at a major conference. I spoke and then he spoke. I sat and listened with no expression on my face, but with a heart of stone. As he spoke, however, something happened. God sovereignly poured His love for this man into my heart. I saw him as a man—a sinner who had been redeemed by Christ, just as I had been a sinner who was redeemed by Christ. I felt warmth and compassion toward him that I had never dreamed possible.

After the evening meeting, I ran into the man in the lobby of the hotel where I was staying. He asked me if I would like to go with him down the street to a cafe to get a bite to eat before retiring for the night. I agreed. We had a wonderful conversation over our late-night snack. I discovered that I had been wrong about him in many ways. God had done some breaking and refining and pruning in his life. He had also done some in mine. We could relate to each other without any animosity whatsoever.

I learned a valuable lesson through that experience. God's love manifests itself in forgiveness—forgiveness that was purchased through sacrifice. What Jesus did for me on the cross, He did for my worst enemy. Therefore, I can't have that person as an enemy. This is what Jesus meant when He taught, "Whenever you stand praying, if you have anything against anyone, forgive him, that your Father in heaven may also forgive you your trespasses. But if you do not forgive, neither will your Father in heaven forgive your trespasses" (Mark 11:25–26 NKJV).

God wants to say to you that His love for you is immeasurable.

God's love for you is inexhaustible and beyond any form of measurement. It cannot be multiplied, added, divided, or subtracted.

Although we never can fully comprehend the vastness of God's love, Paul encouraged the Ephesians to grow in their understanding of God's love:

> *For this reason I bow my knees to the Father of our Lord Jesus Christ . . . that you, being rooted and grounded in love, may be able to comprehend with all the saints what is the width and*

length and depth and height—to know the love of Christ which passes knowledge; that you may be filled with all the fullness of God. (Eph. 3:14, 17–19 NKJV)

As your relationship with God grows deeper, you will find that the Lord reveals to you more and more of His love. You no doubt will find yourself saying again and again, "Lord, I didn't know You could love a person that much. I didn't know it was possible to love like that."

We often discover this truth when other people hurt us. God loves us more than our pain hurts us. He covers our wound with His love. No matter how much others might criticize us, reject us, or cause us harm, if we turn to God in our pain, He extends to us enough love to completely compensate for the pain. We turn to Him with a pound of pain, and He gives us back two pounds of love. He gives us enough love not only to heal us but to provide an overflow of love that we can extend to the very people who hurt us!

The Bible teaches that we are to speak well of our enemies and to do good to them. The expression of our love toward those who harm us will be equal to a heap of hot coals of conviction poured on their heads—in other words, our love will compel them to turn to God for mercy. In this way we overcome evil with good. (See Rom. 12:20–21.)

In recent years, I have experienced a great deal of emotional pain in one particular relationship in my life. It seemed that no matter what I tried to do, I did the wrong thing in this person's eyes. Time after time I went to God, throwing myself on His mercy and love, asking Him to heal my wounds and to help me to respond to this person in the right way. And time after time, I felt His great love pouring over my heart like a healing balm. It was as if He wrapped me in His arms again and again so that He could hold me close and tell me He loved me.

The love God extended to me was in overflow proportions. One of my friends who knew what I was going through said to me, "I don't know how you can speak so calmly about this person. I don't know why you aren't filled with anger. Are you in denial?"

I said, "No, I'm not in denial about the circumstances. I hurt. But I do not hate. I have only love for this person. God gave me an overdose of His love in healing me of my pain, and it's impossible to feel hate when His love has been poured to the overflow point in your heart."

The love that God gives to us is divine love—His love, *agape* love. The love that I felt for this person who had hurt me was not on a human scale. It was an overflow of God's love. And friend, that's the best kind of love there is.

God's Message About His Presence with You

The second great message that God desires to communicate to you on a daily basis is that He is with you—regardless. Again and again, God speaks to your heart, "I'm here."

In communicating His presence to you, the Holy Spirit gives you several specific messages.

He speaks words of affirmation.

The Holy Spirit is 100 percent committed to building you up. The biblical term for this is *edification*—the building up for strength and ministry. The Holy Spirit affirms to you continually that "you belong," "you are worthy," "you are valuable."

Do you have somebody in your life who tells you without qualification or disclaimer, "I believe in you, your talents, your best future"? That person is showing unconditional love to you. The Holy Spirit has this same message for you. He *believes* in you.

One of the foremost assurances that the Holy Spirit gives to you is that you are saved, you are a member of Christ's body. The Holy Spirit brings to your awareness verses of Scripture that affirm to you that you are saved by the atoning blood of Jesus Christ and that when you have believed in Jesus with your heart and confessed your faith in Him with your mouth, you are forever forgiven and assured of eternal life. The Holy Spirit affirms this truth to you. He says to you, "You are cleansed. You are forgiven. You do have eternal life. You do have a home in glory."

He speaks encouragement to give you boldness.

John made this observation: "Love has been perfected among us in this: that we may have boldness in the day of judgment; because as He is, so are we in this world. There is no fear in love; but perfect love casts out fear" (1 John 4:17–18 NKJV).

When Peter and John were imprisoned for healing a man who could not walk and for using that miracle as an opportunity to proclaim the gospel, the authorities who were holding them eventually let them go with a stern threat that they should cease preaching about Jesus.

How did Peter and John respond? They made their way to their fellow believers, reported what the chief priests and elders had said to them, and then they all raised their voices to God with one accord and said,

> *Lord, You are God, who made heaven and earth and the sea, and all that is in them. . . . Now, Lord, look on their threats, and grant to Your servants that with all boldness they may speak Your word, by stretching out Your hand to heal, and that signs and wonders may be done through the name of Your holy Servant Jesus.* (Acts 4:24, 29–30 NKJV)

Peter and John didn't pray against their enemies. They concluded, rather, that "both Herod and Pontius Pilate, with the Gentiles and the people of Israel, were gathered together to do whatever Your hand and Your purpose determined before to be done" (Acts 4:27–28 NKJV). They saw God's hand in their persecution; they saw their affliction as a means of extending the gospel. Therefore, they didn't pray to be released from persecution; rather, they prayed that they might speak even more boldly in the face of it.

When the devil roars against you, don't pray that the roaring will cease; rather, pray that you will have boldness to roar back your witness of the gospel of Jesus Christ with an even greater intensity! God says that He is with you—He will never leave you or forsake you. Furthermore, He is the God of all creation; He has all power and authority. He is on your side. He has a purpose that He will accomplish if you will only replace fear with love and stand strong in His presence.

He gives you a specific word of witness.

Jesus taught His followers, "When they bring you to the synagogues and magistrates and authorities, do not worry about how or what you should answer, or what you should say. For the Holy Spirit will teach you in that very hour what you ought to say" (Luke 12:11–12 NKJV).

On a daily basis, you may not know how to respond to people who ask you questions about your faith. You may be taken by surprise by those who would try to tell you dirty jokes, or who make sarcastic comments against Christians and against God's Word, or who try to talk you into certain activities that you know are contrary to God's commandments. Sometimes people you consider to be friends will tempt you to do what you know not to do. What shall you say?

In these moments you can trust the Holy Spirit to be present with you. You can breathe a quiet prayer, "Help me, Lord. Give me Your words to say." And then you can speak what comes immediately to mind. You can trust the Lord that if you preface your comments with such a prayer, and genuinely are open to hearing what He has to say to you and through you, He will bear the consequences for your words. He will prompt you to speak what He wants you to speak, and He will cause the other person to hear what he or she needs to hear.

He gives you insight into God's eternal plan.

Jesus foretold times of trouble to His followers. He warned His disciples, "They will put you out of the synagogues; yes, the time is coming that whoever kills you will think that he offers God service. And these things they will do to you because they have not known the Father nor Me" (John 16:2–3 NKJV).

Even as Jesus gave His disciples this prophetic word, He added, "When He, the Spirit of truth, has come, He will guide you into all truth; for He will not speak on His own authority, but whatever He hears He will speak; and He will tell you things to come" (John 16:13 NKJV).

There is a big difference between facts and truth. Facts are rooted in details that tell who, what, when, where, and how. Truth, however, encompasses more than facts. It is rooted in *significance* and *meaning*. You can know the facts of an event or situation or experience, but only as you understand the meaning or the significance of what has happened can you come to know the truth. Ultimately, truth has an eternal, divine quality to it. All truth flows from God. All truth points to God. Your quest must be not to get only the facts in life, but to understand life's facts in the context of God's eternal purposes. You must seek to have His understanding and to know what things mean from His perspective.

Truth is what Jesus said the Holy Spirit would give you. He will reveal to you *why* certain things are happening, *how* they fit into the broader purposes of God, and *what* you might expect as a result.

When you are faced with puzzling situations or difficult problems, ask the Lord to reveal to you not only the immediate solution, but also the truth of the matter. Ask Him to tell why He has allowed certain things to happen and what He hopes to accomplish as a result—not only in your life, but in the lives of all others involved directly or indirectly. Jesus said that the Holy Spirit would be faithful in guiding you into all truth.

He gives you direction.

God will reveal the purpose and meaning for things that happen in your life, and He desires to impart wisdom to know how to respond to the things that happen to you. James urged, "If any of you lacks wisdom, let him ask of God, who gives to all liberally and without reproach, and it will be given to him. But let him ask in faith, with no doubting" (James 1:5–6 NKJV).

God does not want you to live in a dark fog, never knowing which way to turn or how to respond to the circumstances that sometimes overwhelm you as tidal waves. No! He wants you to make sound decisions, rational choices, and well-founded plans.

Liberally

God doesn't play games with wisdom. He desires that you know fully what He desires for you to be and do. God has no desire for His people to stumble about in ignorance, wondering if they are acting in a way that is pleasing or displeasing to Him. The Bible is very clear in stating God's commandments and principles. It is very clear in stating God's covenants—what He desires to do for His people and what He requires of His people.

A man was asked, "Do you understand every verse in the Bible?"

"No," he admitted, "but I understand enough of it."

The person asked, "What do you mean 'enough'?"

"Well," the man said, "I understand enough to be troubled. You see, it's not the parts of the Bible that I *don't* understand that trouble me—it's the parts that I *do* understand that trouble me. I understand enough of the Bible to know what I *should* be doing."

The vast majority of people are capable of understanding right from wrong. Their disobedience of God's Word is not the result of a failure to understand the Bible or even a failure to understand the dictates of the God-created conscience; rather, they haven't read the Bible, or they don't want to do what they know they should do.

1. Guidance through His Word, the Bible. If you have a question about the course of action you should take, turn first to your Bible. The Bible is God's foremost way of communicating with you.

In the Bible, you have the complete revelation of God. He doesn't need to add anything else to this Book. Through the ages, the revelation of God was an unfolding truth by God about Himself. In Jesus, that truth was fulfilled. As Jesus said of Himself, He didn't come to change anything about the law or the commandments; He came to show us by His life's example how fully to live out God's plan in our lives and to obey His commandments. (See Matt. 5:17.)

God's Word is for all people because it speaks to the basic human condition. The Bible addresses every emotion, problem of the heart, human relationship dynamic, aspect of the psyche, temptation, desire, heartache, joy, issue of faith, love, or hope that you can experience.

Ask God to speak to you through His Word. In response to your prayer, the Lord often will direct your mind to a particular passage of Scripture that you have encountered in your regular daily reading of the Bible. He will bring to your remembrance His truth on a matter.

If you don't hear from God about precisely where to turn in the Scriptures, begin to read the words of Jesus. (I suggest you read a Bible that has the words of Jesus printed in red ink; that makes it very easy to see what Jesus said.)

You may want to use a concordance to find verses related to a particular problem or question. Many times I have found that God doesn't direct me immediately to the passage that gives me guidance, but as I continue to read and study, God leads me step-by-step to the information that He wants me to see with new spiritual insight.

Eventually, you will come to an incident in Scripture, a passage, or even a single verse that is directly related to your concern, question, or problem.

Of course, you are wise not to limit your search of God's Word to times of extreme need or crisis. Read His Word daily: "This Book of the Law shall not depart from your mouth, but you shall meditate in it day and night, that you may observe to do according to all that is written in it. For then you will make your way prosperous, and then you will have good success" (Josh. 1:8 NKJV).

As you read the Bible daily, God directs you, challenges you, warns you, comforts you, and assures you. Daily reading is like preventive spiritual health care. It's better to divert a problem or to address an issue before it truly becomes a major concern. In daily reading, God refines you, bit by bit, slowly and yet continually transforming your thoughts and responses into those of Jesus.

The guidance that God gives to you in His Word is complete. It is a thorough answer. The more you read the Bible, the more you will begin to see how principles are connected and reinforced. The main themes and teachings of the Bible are repeated again and again—in different words, in different people, in different situations.

2. Guidance from the Holy Spirit. A second way that God speaks to you is through His Holy Spirit, who lives within you. The Holy Spirit brings a "witness" to your spirit that is usually yes or no in nature. The Holy Spirit speaks in your heart a no to everything that will bring you harm; He speaks a yes to everything that will bring you blessing. At times He qualifies His yes to you by saying, "Yes, but first this," or "Yes, but wait." You have a knowing that some might call intuitive. You sense in your spirit His response.

You must ask Him for His guidance. You may make plans and then act on them without submitting them first for His approval and direction. Then when you find yourself in trouble or need, you say, "Why did God allow this? Why me?" The fact is, you never consulted the Lord first about what you were about to do.

You can never ask too many times of the Holy Spirit, "Should I do this—yes or no?" or "Should I say this—yes or no?" Generally speaking, you will have a sense of enthusiasm and eager desire marked with great joy and freedom, or you will have a sense of foreboding, danger, caution, or need for silence.

I find that it is much easier to receive the direction of the Holy Spirit by asking for yes-or-no counsel than to ask Him the broad and undefined question, "What do You want me to do today?" You already have an idea about what needs to be done. Ask the Lord specifically if your wisdom on the matter matches His wisdom—yes or no.

3. Guidance as you pray. Very often, in imparting wisdom to you, the Holy Spirit will remind you of what God has said to you and done for you in the past. Sometimes He will give you very detailed words to say or very clear directions about where to go and what to do. At times He will guide you as you pray.

On countless occasions, I have not started out to pray for a certain thing, but as I have waited in silence for the Holy Spirit to bring to my mind various aspects of a situation, I find that He reveals things to me, and I feel prompted to pray in a direction I had not anticipated.

4. Guidance through godly advice from other people. In addition to speaking to you through His Word and through the Holy Spirit, God uses other people to speak to you. Some may be total strangers. Others may be members of your immediate family or friends. He uses pastors, teachers, and Bible study group leaders.

As you open yourself up to hear God's word from other people, make certain that the word they give to you is in total alignment with God's written Word. God doesn't forget what He has already said, and He doesn't contradict Himself. If a word is from God, it will be consistent with what God has already revealed through Scripture and in the life of His Son, the Lord Jesus Christ. Also make certain that the person who gives you counsel has no ulterior personal motive. When you are confused, in pain, or in dire need, you are much more subject to manipulation than you might be at other times. Make certain that the person doesn't want something from you, isn't trying to manipulate you for personal purposes, or isn't seeking personal praise and glory for the counsel given.

God's word through other people will never be anything that might harm another person. If someone advises you to take action that will damage or destroy another person's reputation, relationships, spiritual growth, or property, don't take that advice. God's word is for your ultimate and eternal good but also for the ultimate and eternal good of all His children.

Listen for two or more witnesses. The Lord may direct you to two or more passages of the Bible that convey the same meaning. He may bring a total stranger across your path who speaks a word that is very close to what you heard from your pastor in last Sunday's sermon. He may use a scriptural song that you hear on the radio to confirm what a friend counseled you to do. God gives His wisdom *liberally*. He desires to make Himself known to you and to reveal the full extent of what He desires for you.

Without Reproach

God never offers His guidance to you with the attitude, "You are stupid for asking this," or "You ought to know better." God never shames you for not having His wisdom. The heavenly Father doesn't impart His wisdom with reproach; rather, He instructs you as a patient teacher instructs a cherished student.

If you don't understand God clearly, He will speak to you again and again—using one method and then the next—to get His message across to you. As long as you seek to follow His guidance, He continues to send you His messages of wise counsel.

Reproach is a tool of the enemy. Satan says, "You'll never be a good person," "You've sinned to the point that God can never forgive you," "You've made so many mistakes that God can't use you anymore," "You're never going to get this right," "You can't give up this bad habit so quit trying," or "You are unworthy of God's love."

The devil lies to you about your ability to receive and understand God's wisdom, or your ability to enact it in practical ways in your life.

The reproach of the enemy often couches itself in terms of timing: "If you don't take action right now, you'll miss out," or "If you act now, people will think you are impetuous; wait a while." The reproach is this: you can't know God's timing.

A part of God's wisdom imparted to you will be not only *what* to do, but also *how* to do it and *when* to do it. Be sure to wait for the Lord to give you His full counsel on a matter. He will reveal to you the methods you are to use, even the tone of voice you are to use, and He will show you when to act. David knew this well. Time and time again he inquired of the Lord about what to do, how to do it, and when to take action. He said, "My soul, wait silently for God alone, / For my expectation is from Him" (Ps. 62:5 NKJV).

There are times when the Lord will tell you to wait.

There may be things that the Lord needs to do in another person's life before He can fulfill His plans in your life. There are other times when the Lord will tell you, "Act now. Don't delay." Be sensitive to His timing. The Lord wants you to be effective and successful in carrying out His will. He does not believe you are incapable of discerning His methods and timing.

Once you have heard from God, do what He tells you to do without doubting and without hesitating.

He speaks words of peace to your heart.

Even as the Lord gives you boldness, He gives you calm. Have you ever experienced this in your life? You knew what had to be done, and you knew you were the person to do it, and along with the courage you felt, you also felt a great sense of inner calm that come what may, you had to act. That's the peace of God, which is always attendant with God's abiding presence. It's a peace that says, "I know God is in charge of my life and this moment. Come what may, I belong to the Lord, and He is present with me."

Paul wrote to the Philippians these words of comfort:

Be anxious for nothing, but in everything by prayer and sup-
plication, with thanksgiving, let your requests be made known
to God; and the peace of God, which surpasses all understanding,
will guard your hearts and minds through Christ Jesus. (Phil.
4:6–7 NKJV)

Keep in mind that Paul wrote that letter from a Roman prison.
He had been in Roman custody for years. He never knew from one
day to the next what his fate would be—from Rome's standpoint.
Paul always knew, however, what his fate would be from God's standpoint.

He had confidence that God was in charge and that God would
continue to be in charge until his last breath on this earth, and even
then, God would continue to be in charge of his life. Therefore, Paul
could make his requests to God with thanksgiving—he could ask
for what he desired and, at the same time, thank God that God was
in charge and God's will would be done. The ability to pray with
thanksgiving gave Paul a deep peace, a total lack of anxiety or worry.

Do you know a person who is always fretting, always worry-
ing, always upset about what to do or what will happen? That person may even be you.

The antidote for worry is a greater awareness of God's presence. When you feel anxiety rising up in you, ask God to make
His presence known to you. Let Him know that you are trusting
in Him. Tell Him what you would like to see happen, but add to
your petition thanks for what God has done in your life in the past
and praise for who God is. The more you thank and praise God, the
greater calm you will experience. He is the Lord of all! All things
do come from Him! He is our Provider, our Deliverer, our Savior,
our Redeemer, our Rock, our Fortress, our Truth, our Life. He is the
King of the universe, and He is still on His eternal throne.

And then, having made your petition known to God with
thanksgiving and praise, choose to think about something other

than your problem. It is no accident that Paul followed up his words about being anxious for nothing by saying,

> *Whatever things are true, whatever things are noble, whatever things are just, whatever things are pure, whatever things are lovely, whatever things are of good report, if there is any virtue and if there is anything praiseworthy—meditate on these things.* (Phil. 4:8 NKJV)

Turn your attention away from your problem and toward the things that are truly good. Turn your mind to the solutions and answers that God has given you in the past. Turn your mind to His blessings and His promises. Focus your mind on His goodness and His love for you.

And then Paul advised, "The things which you learned and received and heard and saw in me, these do" (Phil. 4:9 NKJV).

Having prayed with thanksgiving and praise, and having turned your mind toward what is of God and from God, you must then begin to do what God leads you to do. Paul said, "Do what I have done." And what did Paul do? He worked; he prayed; he gave his witness; he taught the Scriptures to those who wanted to learn. He stayed very busy doing good things that were of benefit to himself, others, and, ultimately, the kingdom of God.

That pattern of praying, focusing on the positive, and doing good is one that Paul said will cause you to be keenly aware that "the God of peace will be with you" (Phil. 4:9 NKJV).

He tells you His presence with you is abiding.

How often can you ask God for boldness, insight, or direction? As many times as necessary. He is always available. The Holy Spirit does not make periodic visitations to your life. No—He *abides* with you. He dwells within you. Jesus said, "He who abides in Me, and I in him, bears much fruit" (John 15:5 NKJV).

You can trust God to give you boldness and wisdom that are effective. You'll bear fruit. You'll get the job done that God wants done. Along the way, you'll have an understanding of what God is seeking to accomplish in you and through you. You'll have the peace and calm of His presence. The Holy Spirit does not come and go from your life. He is with you *always*.

God's Message to You About Heaven

God has a third message for you, and the message is about your future and your ultimate destiny.

One of God's greatest acts of love toward us is the creation of heaven for us as our eternal home. God doesn't merely love us enough to create us and give us several decades of life on this earth. He loves us for all eternity. He intends to spend forever with us.

Jesus said to His disciples,

Let not your heart be troubled; you believe in God, believe also in Me. In My Father's house are many mansions; if it were not so, I would have told you. I go to prepare a place for you. And if I go and prepare a place for you, I will come again and receive you to Myself; that where I am, there you may be also. (John 14:1–3 NKJV)

Isn't it wonderful to know that Jesus is preparing a place just for *you*? If Jesus is preparing it, it's bound to be good—even beyond your highest expectations. A man told me, "I don't know what kind of place Jesus is preparing for me, but He's been preparing it for nearly two thousand years now and it only took Him seven days to make the world, so whatever kind of place it is, I know it's going to be far more wonderful than anything I could ever imagine!" Paul no doubt felt that way when he wrote to the Ephesians, "Now to Him who is able to do exceedingly abundantly above all that we ask or think" (Eph. 3:20 NKJV).

Paul wrote very specifically to the Colossians about heaven:

We give thanks to the God and Father of our Lord Jesus Christ, praying always for you, since we heard of your faith in Christ Jesus and of your love for all the saints; because of the hope which is laid up for you in heaven, of which you heard before in the word of the truth of the gospel. (Col. 1:3–5 NKJV)

What is the hope of heaven?

First and foremost, it is the hope of being with God for all eternity. It is the hope of everlasting life in the direct presence of your Creator.

Second, it is the hope that your life will come to full fruition. All that you have done, said, and been in this life will be revealed and judged by God. For the believer in Christ Jesus this judgment is nothing to be feared. Rather, it is something to anticipate with joy. Heaven is the place where you will be rewarded for your faithfulness.

This hope of heaven has a purifying effect on your life. When heaven and the rewards of God are kept in sharp focus before you, you have an increased desire and commitment to live as God intends for you to live—you want to give your best effort to saying and doing all that God asks you to say and do. The hope of heaven compels you to grow, yield to God's transformation work in your life, and become the person He has destined you to be. When you look around, you easily can become discouraged and feel as if you have failed to succeed according to the standards of the world. When you look toward Jesus and toward your eternal life in your heavenly home, you have a sense of encouragement and a feeling that you *are* succeeding according to God's standards.

Third, the hope of heaven is a life that is totally separated from evil. In heaven, there is no shadow, no darkness, no negative presence. In John's vision of heaven, he heard a voice from heaven proclaiming, "God will wipe away every tear from their eyes; there shall be no more death, nor sorrow, nor crying. There shall be no more pain, for the former things have passed away" (Rev. 21:4 NKJV).

Whatever you envision as being of greatest quality, most noble character, and brightest beauty, that is what you will experience in heaven, for you will be in the presence of God and those who are filled with the Spirit of God, without any influence of sin or the weaknesses of the flesh.

The Reason to Know About Heaven

God desires to say more to you about heaven. How do I know that to be true? Because there is much about heaven that God desires to see each one of us bring to this earth through our prayers, words, and actions.

Jesus taught His disciples to pray,

> *Your kingdom come.*
> *Your will be done*
> *On earth as it is in heaven.* (Matt. 6:10 NKJV)

What exactly are you praying? If you don't have an understanding about heaven, and about God's rule of heaven, God's methods in heaven, God's purposes in heaven, how can you know if God's will is being done on this earth?

We are not destined to live solely on this earth. Our true home is heaven. We are citizens of heaven, and therefore, we are to abide by the higher laws and commandments of heaven. We are only travelers through this life. Paul called us "fellow citizens with the saints" and "ambassadors for Christ." (See Eph. 2:19; 2 Cor. 5:20 [NKJV].) We are Christ's emissaries on this earth—our true loyalty is to heaven.

God desires to reveal more to you about your eternal home so you will know better how to live in your temporary home—this earth.

What are some of the hallmarks of heaven?

Praise

John told us in his revelation that the throne of God is surrounded continually by those who praise God. They cry day and night,

> *Holy, holy, holy,*
> *Lord God Almighty,*
> *Who was and is and is to come! . . .*
> *You are worthy, O Lord,*
> *To receive glory and honor and power;*
> *For You created all things,*
> *And by Your will they exist and were created.* (Rev. 4:8, 11 NKJV)

When you praise God on earth, you are rehearsing something that you will be doing forever. Surely, a major part of your bringing heaven to earth is accomplished through and manifested by praise.

The Exaltation of Jesus

Those who offer praise in heaven also proclaim the worthiness of Jesus. They cry out about our Lord,

> *You are worthy to take the scroll,*
> *And to open its seals;*
> *For You were slain,*
> *And have redeemed us to God by Your blood*
> *Out of every tribe and tongue and people and nation,*
> *And have made us kings and priests to our God;*
> *And we shall reign on the earth. . . .*
> *Worthy is the Lamb who was slain*
> *To receive power and riches and wisdom,*
> *And strength and honor and glory and blessing! . . .*
> *Blessing and honor and glory and power*
> *Be to Him who sits on the throne,*
> *And to the Lamb, forever and ever!* (Rev. 5:9–10, 12, 13 NKJV)

Your purpose as a Christian on this earth is to raise up Jesus, who said, "As Moses lifted up the serpent in the wilderness, even so must the Son of Man be lifted up, that whoever believes in Him should not perish but have eternal life" (John 3:14–15 NKJV). He also said, "I, if I am lifted up from the earth, will draw all peoples to Myself" (John 12:32 NKJV).

Jesus was prophesying His death on the cross, but the fact is, when you call people's attention to the cross and to the sacrifice that Jesus made there, He draws sinners to Himself as their Savior. Your purpose is to do the exalting of Jesus. Again, this is something you will be doing throughout eternity. This is a way you bring heaven to earth.

The Humility to Serve and Authority to Reign

John said of God's servants in heaven, "And His servants shall serve Him. . . . And they shall reign forever and ever" (Rev. 22:3, 5 NKJV).

Part of what you do in bringing God's kingdom of heaven to earth is realized when you serve others—when you meet their needs, affirm them, teach them God's ways, and minister to them the gifts of the Holy Spirit as He pours these gifts through you as His vessel. You serve others when you proclaim the gospel of Jesus to them and make them disciples of the Lord, eager to obey His commands and follow in His footsteps. Your service to others is to be open and pure, without any shadow of ill motive.

Every servant has a master. Paul wrote to the Ephesians that the Master is in heaven (Eph. 6:9). You are to be quick to do His bidding.

As you serve, you are also to reign—not over people, but over evil. With Christ's love motivating you and the Holy Spirit empowering you, you are called to serve people and have dominion over the powers of Satan. So many people get this backward—they are ruling over people and serving Satan. Your role as a believer in Christ and disciple of the Lord is the exact opposite. You are to model for others the way that Jesus lived His life—a life of daily ministry to those in need, and a life of total victory over the power of the devil. You are to have full power and authority over the enemy, using the name of Jesus as you withstand the devil's assaults, resist his temptations, and endure any trials he may send your way. (See Eph. 6:9–10; James 4:7; 1:12.)

There is much more that the Lord seeks to reveal to you about heaven, but this much is certain: the Holy Spirit's guidance of your life is in full accord with the "operations manual" of heaven. He has heaven in mind as your destiny, and His efforts are all aimed at guarding your steps and guiding your way so that you walk a straight path to your eternal home.

Are You Listening?

God has much to say to you each day—about His great love, about the way He desires for you to live and experience His presence, about your ultimate destination. The question you must ask yourself is, Am I listening?

God is always speaking. The problem in your communication with God does not lie with Him. It lies in your lack of interest, your inability to hear Him clearly, and your failure to take the time to listen to all that He longs to say to you.

In telling you of His love for you, God gives you motivation to face life with faith and enthusiasm.

In telling you of His plans, giving His guidance, and imparting His presence, God gives you a great sense of security and purpose.

In telling you of your future home, God gives you His goal for your life.

With love in your heart, ideas and plans and truth in your mind, and a goal for your efforts, you can't help having hope! You are eager to hear more of what God has to say. And the good news is that God always has more that He desires to share with you, to reveal to you, and to impart to you so that you might be comforted, guided, and perfected.

Yes, indeed, you have reason to make this statement of hope:

I have hope because God still has more that He desires to say to me!

CHAPTER 6

GOD STILL HAS A NEED FOR YOU TO MEET

Who *needs* you?

Who will be worse off if you don't show up in their lives today?

You may feel as if nobody needs you, nobody cares whether you are alive. But let me assure you of this: *somebody* on the earth needs you. You may not have met that person (or those people) yet, but somebody is desperate for your love, care, and talents.

I once met with a woman whose husband had died a few months earlier. She had been a Christian for quite some time, but she was devastated by her husband's death. He had done everything for her. She had virtually no skills to take care of herself. She didn't know how to write a check or drive a car. About the only thing she knew how to do was to shop for groceries and fix meals. She said, "When my husband died, my world fell apart. Without him, there just isn't any life."

She began to sob. She admitted, "I've been having one of those pity parties you talk about ever since my husband died. My mother has talked to me about my getting on with my life, my friends have tried to encourage me, but nothing's working. I try to tell myself that things will get better, but they aren't getting better. I try to pray, but I feel as if the words are just echoing around the empty house. I feel helpless. I feel hopeless. I'm depressed."

I knew enough about her situation to know that her husband had left her with financial means so that she had no worries about meeting the basic needs in her life. But still, she felt she had no purpose, no direction, no meaning to her life.

She finally concluded, "I came to ask you, Do I have a reason for living?"

I let her talk and cry herself out, and then I said, "Let's think about this for a minute." She calmed a bit.

I asked her if she had accepted Jesus as her Savior. She said she had. I asked her when she had done that, and she told me that it had been a number of years ago. "Well," I asked, "are you still saved? Is Jesus still in your life?"

She said, "Yes . . . ," then proceeded to give me a number of "buts."

I said, "Now wait a minute. Is He in your life, or isn't He?"

She said, "Yes, He's in my life," and then she went right on with another "but" and continued with a description of how bad things had been for her in recent months.

I said, "Has Jesus changed?"

"No."

"Do you believe His promises? Are His promises still true?"

"Yes." Again, "But I feel so hopeless and so helpless. What am I supposed to do in my life?"

I said, "Here's the way I look at life. If you are going to enjoy life, you need someone to love and someone to feel loved by. You need something to live for, something that grabs your attention and is bigger than you are. You need to be able to laugh at something. You need somebody to lean on."

This time she didn't come back at me with any "buts." She listened intently. I continued, "You have God to lean on. He's there. He hasn't changed or moved away. You can count on Him. He loves you. So does your mother. So do your children and your friends.

From what you've told me, you have some things in your life that are good for a laugh or two. Now what you need to start doing is to focus on someone to love, and something that is bigger than yourself to live for. You need to start reaching out beyond yourself and start giving something of yourself to someone else."

"Do you mean money?" she asked.

"No," I said. "I mean something of *you*. If you get committed to something that requires money or if the Lord leads you to get involved in a project that needs money, He'll show you what to give in that area. I'm talking primarily, however, about giving something of yourself to somebody in need."

"I don't feel as if I have anything to give," she said candidly.

"Sure you do," I encouraged her. "Everybody has something to give. You have time you can give—even if it is to sit with somebody in a rest home or a hospital. You have lots of talents to give. You may not have discovered all your talents because your husband did so many things for you and made so many of the decisions that related to your life, but you are an intelligent, educated, and talented woman. You have abilities you have never tapped into. The main thing is to make yourself available."

She agreed to give some thought to what she might be capable of giving to someone—a person or perhaps an organization in need of volunteers. I gave her the names of several people who could use a willing person to help out in tangible, important ways that were not overly demanding emotionally.

I said, "In choosing a place to give yourself away, you are also going to be putting yourself into a position to find somebody to love."

She quickly said, "I don't think I'll ever fall in love again. My husband was my only true love."

"That isn't what I mean," I said. "There are lots of lonely people in this world who need love—not romantic love, but the love of friendship or the divine *agape* love of God. Look around. There's somebody you know, or somebody you will meet in the course of your giving of your time and talents, whom you will recognize as being a person truly in need of love."

I could tell she was considering this carefully. Some of her "buts" still echoed in my mind—including her great need to feel loved. "You are feeling right now that *you* are the one who is in need of love," I said. "Isn't that right?"

She nodded.

"And you are," I said. "I'm not overlooking your need at all. The way you are going to have the need for love met in your own life is to give love. When we give, we open ourselves to receive. We always receive more from the Lord than we give away."

I opened my Bible to Luke 6:38 (NKJV) and handed it to her to read aloud: "Give, and it will be given to you: good measure, pressed down, shaken together, and running over will be put into your bosom. For with the same measure that you use, it will be measured back to you."

"I thought that was about money," she said after she had read the verse aloud.

"There's no mention of money in that verse," I said. "In fact, that verse is part of a longer passage of Jesus' teaching that is about loving other people and giving to them—a passage that is about doing good to others, even our enemies, and showing mercy and forgiveness to others. When you give love, you are in a position to receive overwhelming, abundant, generous, flowing-over-the-top love."

She said, "Where do I go to find somebody to love?"

I said, "First, find a place where you can serve others in the name of Jesus. Get involved in an outreach ministry of some kind that is helping other people who are in need. Since you are lonely right now, I suggest you join with other Christians in helping with a project that is bigger than what any person can do alone. Get involved."

"I don't know if I have the strength to do this," she said.

"In all likelihood, you don't," I said. Then I turned in my Bible to Philippians 4:13 (NKJV) and again handed my Bible to her so she could read this verse for herself: "I can do all things through Christ who strengthens me."

"You can trust Christ to help you," I said. "Even before you get out of bed in the morning, ask Him to give you the strength to get up, get dressed, and get moving. Ask Him to help you do just one thing every day that will be of help to just one other person. I'm not asking you to take on the world. I'm encouraging you to get involved in some way, every day, in helping to show love to just one other person who needs to know that God cares about him or her."

I paused for a moment, and when she didn't say anything, I added, "What do you have to lose? You're already miserable and without any hope. It doesn't seem to me that you can get any lower than you already are. You said you didn't want to go on this way. Why not give this a try? Trust God to help you, and then make an effort every day to do something to help or show love to another person."

I sensed that she was just about out of "buts." She said, "All right. I'll give it a try."

We had prayer together and she left. I didn't hear directly from her for several weeks. I did ask a couple of people about her and learned through the grapevine that she had volunteered to assist in the childcare center answering the phone and making sandwiches for the children's lunch. Then I heard that she had also volunteered to help with a feeding program for street people. My guess is that when she discovered that making sandwiches was a form of ministry that she could do easily, she also volunteered to help make and distribute sandwiches at the early morning food line.

A couple of months went by, and then I ran into her after a church service. The look on her face told me her story even before she opened her mouth. "It's gone," she said to me. "All that depression. The darkness lifted. I don't know exactly what happened, but I realized one morning that it was just gone."

"Have you found someone to whom you can give your love and care?" I asked.

"Oh, yes," she said, and then she added in a very serious tone of voice, almost as if she was telling me a secret, "Pastor, there are more people in this city who need love than anybody knows. There are some people with real *needs*. I may not be able to do a lot of the big jobs, but I've found that there are a great many little jobs that I can do—jobs that need doing and people who need helping."

"The more you give, the more you receive," I encouraged her, recalling our conversation.

She said, "That's certainly true. I don't think I've ever been this busy in my whole life. I don't have time to be depressed! But you know, I'm the one who is receiving so much. It's just as you said. The more you give, the more you receive."

She was beaming as she spoke. You could see the joy on her face. "And you have hope back in your life?" I asked.

"Oh, my, yes!" she said. "There's a lot that still needs to be done, and I'm convinced that I can help do it!"

Your Need to Give Love to Others

One of the great love stories in the Bible is found in Luke 15:11–24 (NKJV). It is perhaps the most famous of all Jesus' parables. Even if you know this story, I encourage you to read it again:

A certain man had two sons. And the younger of them said to his father, "Father, give me the portion of goods that falls to me." So he divided to them his livelihood. And not many days after, the younger son gathered all together, journeyed to a far country, and there wasted his possessions with prodigal living. But when he had spent all, there arose a severe famine in that land, and he began to be in want. Then he went and joined himself to a citizen of that country, and he sent him into his fields to feed swine. And he would gladly have filled his stomach with the pods that the swine ate, and no one gave him anything. But when he came to himself, he said, "How many of my father's hired servants have bread enough and to spare, and I perish with hunger! I will arise and go to my father, and will say to him, 'Father, I have sinned against heaven and before you, and I am no longer worthy to be called your son. Make me like one of your hired servants.' " And he arose and came to his father. But when he was still a great way off, his father saw him and had compassion, and ran and fell on his neck and kissed him. And the son said to him, "Father, I have sinned against heaven and in your sight, and am no longer worthy to be called your son." But the father said to his servants, "Bring out the best robe and put it on him, and put a ring on his hand and sandals on his feet. And bring the fatted calf here and kill it, and let us eat and be merry; for this my son was dead and is alive again; he was lost and is found." And they began to be merry.

This parable of Jesus is often called the parable of the prodigal son. In my opinion, it should be called the parable of the loving father. The story is not so much about the son who turned his back on his father and fell into sin, but about the father who continued to love his son and fully accepted him back into his family.

This is the last of three stories and teachings that Jesus gave in Luke 15. In the first story, a man has a hundred sheep. He loses one of them and leaves the other ninety-nine sheep to go in search of the one he has lost until he finds it. He returns home rejoicing and calls upon his friends and neighbors to rejoice with him.

In the second story, Jesus told about a woman who has ten silver coins—very likely the coins of a headdress that was her dowry—and she loses one of the coins. She sweeps and searches her entire house until she finds it, and just like the shepherd who returns with the lost sheep, she calls her friends and neighbors and says, "Rejoice with me, for I have found the piece that I lost."

In both stories, Jesus said, "There is joy in the presence of the angels of God over those who repent." (See Luke 15:1–10.)

What do these three stories tell us about the love of God?

First, God is committed in His love.

God extends Himself to those He loves. He goes after those who turn away from Him.

People often seem to think that God has turned His back on them or given up on them. The very opposite is true. The shepherd goes after his one lost sheep. The woman searches for her one lost coin. The loving father is looking for his son; otherwise he wouldn't see him while he is still a great way off. He runs and falls on his son's neck and kisses him.

God's arms are always open wide, extended to those who have turned from Him. He is committed to love regardless of what happens.

Second, God desires your best.

A sure sign of committed love is this: a person wants what is best for the loved one.

I heard recently about a young man who was very much in love with a young woman he had met in college. He had dated her for more than a year and had every intention of marrying her. Just a few months, however, before he had planned to present her with an engagement ring, she went on a short-term missions trip as part of one of her college classes. Her trip dramatically affected her life, and she decided that God might be calling her to be a missionary.

The young man said, "I don't feel the call she feels, and I hate the idea of giving her up, but I love her enough to say to her, 'I want God's best in your life.' If God's best is for her to be a missionary, then she needs to be a missionary."

Giving up his relationship with the young woman was the most difficult thing he has done in his life. At the same time, he has peace. He said not too long ago, "I know that whatever happens, God wants what is best for her *and* for me. I've got great hope that things are going to work out OK . . . maybe not in the way I had thought and hoped and dreamed about a few months ago, but things are going to work out for good. God is in charge of both of our lives, and He's not going to lead either one of us into something that is bad for us."

The loving father in Jesus' parable could have made his returning son a servant. That is what the son requested. That certainly would have been what the boy's older brother would have desired. It would have been what might be expected of the father by the community in which he lived. Nobody would have condemned the father for refusing to accept his son or for making his son a servant in his household. But that wasn't the position the father took. He wanted what was best for his boy—and nothing but the best. The best was to be a son, a full member of the family.

Third, God's love is always affirming.

God tells you repeatedly in His Word, "You belong. You are worthy. You are My child. I am your God. I believe in you, your talents, and your future." The loving father in Jesus' parable never ceased calling his son "son." He stated that his son "was dead and is alive again; he was lost and is found," but the father never stopped believing that his son was going to come home and be his son once again.

Fourth, God does everything you will allow Him to do to build you up.

Throughout God's Word, we find the Lord giving to His people to build them up and make them great. *Their* turning away to other gods or discounting God or seeking to do things their own way results in their chastisement. God doesn't take from men and women; He doesn't draw His strength, power, or glory by stripping these things from His creation. No! The exact opposite is true. He gives His strength, power, and wisdom to humankind, freely and liberally. He gave His beloved Son to redeem humankind on the cross. He gives generously from the infinite storehouse of blessings in heaven to reward His people.

God asks only that we turn to Him, receive His forgiveness, and seek to obey Him. When we do, He opens the floodgates of blessing in our direction.

The prophet Malachi spoke to a generation of Hebrews who had turned away from God's commandments. They were no longer bringing their sacrifices and gifts to the temple. As a result, the entire nation was suffering, and so was the ongoing worship in the temple. Malachi called the people back to obedient giving with this word from the Lord:

> *"Bring all the tithes into the storehouse,*
> *That there may be food in My house,*
> *And try Me now in this,"*
> *Says the* Lord *of hosts,*
> *"If I will not open for you the windows of heaven*
> *And pour out for you such blessing*
> *That there will not be room enough to receive it.*
> *And I will rebuke the devourer for your sakes,*
> *So that he will not destroy the fruit of your ground,*
> *Nor shall the vine fail to bear fruit for you in the field,"*
> *Says the* Lord *of hosts;*
> *"And all nations will call you blessed,*
> *For you will be a delightful land,"*
> *Says the* Lord *of hosts.* (Mal. 3:10–12 NKJV)

What an amazing blessing is promised to those who obey! God asks them only to obey His commandments, to give one-tenth of their produce and earnings to Him. He gives back a blessing that is so great, they can't contain it. Their crops will produce in abundance. They will be a delightful nation, the envy of all other nations.

But that isn't all.

At the time of Malachi the people also were speaking harshly against God, saying, "It is useless to serve God" (Mal. 3:14 NKJV). The people were praising those who were disobedient and proud against God.

Malachi said that the Lord had a

> *book of remembrance . . .*
> *For those who fear the LORD*
> *And who meditate on His name.* (Mal. 3:16 NKJV)

And read what he said of those in the book,

> *"They shall be Mine," says the LORD of hosts,*
> *"On the day that I make them My jewels.*
> *And I will spare them*
> *As a man spares his own son who serves him. . . .*
> *For behold, the day is coming,*
> *Burning like an oven,*
> *And all the proud, yes, all who do wickedly will be stubble. . . .*
> *That will leave them neither root nor branch.*
> *But to you who fear My name*
> *The Sun of Righteousness shall arise*
> *With healing in His wings;*
> *And you shall go out*
> *And grow fat like stall-fed calves."* (Mal. 3:17, 4:2 NKJV)

God asks only that His people be obedient to His commandments. His blessings to them for obedience are life, healing, and prosperity of spirit. He calls the obedient ones His "jewels"—His special treasure.

You may think the Lord asks a lot of you, but in the context of all eternity and the infinity of the universe, He asks so little. In return for your halting, imperfect, sometimes wavering obedience, He gives you everything that you can ever count as vital or valuable.

God is the One who gives you life. He alone numbers beats of your heart and gives you each breath you take.

God is the One who gives you health and who causes healing to occur in your body when it has been injured or attacked by disease. He alone can cause your body to function in the way He created it.

God is the One who puts you into a family and relationships that are for your benefit.

God is the One who gives you creative ideas for good and then imparts to you the courage to do them. He is the One who enables you by the power of His Holy Spirit to discern evil from good and to make wise choices.

God is the One who causes joy to well up in your spirit and who leads you into paths of righteousness.

God is the One who saves your soul and cleanses you from sin and promises you eternal life with Him.

The Bible tells us very little about God, apart from how generous God is to His people and how diligently He guards them, provides for them, and keeps them from being overwhelmed by evil.

What we know about the loving father in this parable of Jesus is primarily what he *did* for his son. We don't know what the father did for a living. We don't know what chores he gave his son to do. But we do know that he gave his younger son the inheritance that he requested, he greeted his son with open arms when he returned home, he gave him back all the marks of sonship—a robe, a ring, and sandals—and he ordered a celebration to be given in honor of his return. The father did everything within his power to build up his son and restore him fully to what he considered to be his rightful place.

The Portrait of Unconditional Love

In the parable of the loving father, we have a portrait of God and a definition of unconditional love:

- Unconditional love is committed.
- Unconditional love desires the best for others.
- Unconditional love is affirming.
- Unconditional love builds up others.

God desires that you give this brand of love to other people. The fact is, everybody needs this kind of love. And too few people give it.

In an article I read about world hunger, the statistics given regarding the amount of hunger in the world were staggering. In our nation of plenty, we can easily lose sight of the fact that the majority of people in the world will not have sufficient food today (this day and every day), or they have no storehouse of food to ensure that they will eat tomorrow. The majority of the world's people are always hungry and are never far from the threat of starvation. Not only do tens of thousands of people die daily of starvation, but tens of thousands more are ill with diseases related to lack of food.

And yet, there is sufficient food production in the world to feed all of the people on the planet. World hunger is a matter not of food production, but of food distribution, and in most cases, food distribution is subjected to the "politics of hate." In most of the places afflicted by starvation, one group of people (generally those in power) doesn't want another group of people to have sufficient food. At its root, hunger is a "heart matter." People don't care enough, don't love enough, and aren't committed enough in their love to feed their neighbors or allow them to be fed.

If every person on the planet awoke tomorrow morning and said, "I'm going to be committed to doing what I can to help others. I desire to see my neighbors fed. I believe my neighbors are valuable, worthy, and important to God and to my nation. And I'm going to do what I can to build them up rather than destroy them," world hunger would be eradicated within a matter of hours or days.

The same goes for wars—including disputes within the office, family, or church.

The same goes for problems that arise from racial tensions or disagreements among religious persuasions.

Unconditional love is never based upon a person's worthiness to receive love; rather, it is an act of the will.

In my opinion, we express unconditional love *only* when we acknowledge that we are the recipients of that brand of love from God. Freely we have received, and freely we must give. We must forget forever the word *deserve* in association with love.

Meeting Needs Out of a Heart That LovesUnconditionally

Why this concern for the nature of unconditional love? Because God desires for you to start giving of yourself with unconditional love to meet the needs of other people.

There are six hallmarks of the way you are to give love and care to others:

1. Acceptance

The loving father *ran* to his son on sight. The movement toward another person is a sign of acceptance. The father did not wait to see what his son looked like or what his son had to say. He ran to him regardless of his son's condition. His was an unconditional love expressed with unconditional acceptance.

God is always in a stance of acceptance toward His children. Anytime you are ready to turn to Him, He is ready to receive you. He accepts you as you are.

Surely, the desire of every parent is to see his child live up to his potential, love God, and do good in life. But the stance of the parent who loves unconditionally must be one of love without qualification. The parent can encourage the child to be and do his best, present the child with the gospel in both example and teaching, and train the child to do what is right. But no parent can control or determine the outcome of the child's life. That is a matter of the child's will and of the child's relationship with God. Encouraging is different from loving conditionally. The parent who loves conditionally says, "I will love you only if you do certain things." To encourage with unconditional love is to say, "I love you because you are my child. I encourage you to be and do your best for *your* sake, not mine."

The parent who puts conditions on love wants the child to do or be certain things so the parent will look good. The parent who loves unconditionally wants the child to be and do whatever God leads the child to be and do, so that the child will be blessed and God will receive the honor and praise for His work in the child's life. The motivations are very different.

Acceptance is manifested in many ways, mostly by your saying to another person, "Come be with me." Go with me on this errand, walk with me on our way to a place we both need to go, sit with me a while, or come over and visit. A person feels acceptance anytime you set another place at the table for her, are willing to include her in your plan, or invite her to be a part of your group.

I heard about a child who was adopted into a family when he was ten years old. He was having a little difficulty feeling truly accepted by his new family until the day came when his father said to him, "Here's your set of chores." He said, "When I knew that I had been given certain responsibilities, just like all the other kids, I knew I was on my way to being accepted." Then he added, "But I knew I was fully accepted when my dad punished me for failing to complete my chores. He punished me just the same as he did the other kids when they failed to do their chores—no dessert that night and no watching TV until the job was done the next day. That's when I knew I was really a part of the family." Acceptance means being included into a group, with the same status, same rules, same consequences, same treatment.

Showing acceptance means treating a person just as you would like to be treated.

Anytime you seek to give love and care to another person, you must examine your motives and ask, Am I willing to accept this person just as she is?

2. Touching

Upon reaching his son, the loving father in Jesus' parable embraced him and kissed him.

Consider the state of the boy. He had been traveling. But not only that, he had wasted all of his inheritance in "prodigal living." He had then experienced famine. And at his lowest point, he had gone to work feeding swine "and would gladly have filled his stomach with the pods that the swine ate." The boy no doubt looked and smelled like the hogs he had been tending. He was wasted away with sinful living and the hunger of famine. To the father, the boy no doubt looked like only a shadow of his former self. From a strict Jewish standpoint, the boy was unclean—a sinner. Of course, Jesus was telling the parable to the Pharisees and scribes, who had been very critical of Jesus' willingness to talk to and eat with sinners.

In the Jewish religious law, touching an unclean person made a person unclean also, and he was to be "separated" from the righteous until he went through certain rituals for cleansing.

The loving father was willing to become unclean. He was willing to touch his son even if it meant that he would be temporarily separated—perhaps even ridiculed or criticized—for his actions.

Our heavenly Father touched all of humankind in sending His Son, Jesus, to this earth. He mingled with sinners. He walked where we walk and did the things that we human beings do. He totally identified with our humanity. Jesus was fully human, even though He was also fully divine.

The sense of touch is one of the most powerful senses related to emotional well-being and mental health. Children who don't receive sufficient touching have a greatly increased probability of developing psychological disorders in which they become detached from humanity and have an inability to make commitments or to enjoy satisfactory relationships with other people.

Touch has been linked to physical healing. Several research studies reported in recent years have shown that touching seems to be related to a patient's rate of progress after surgery or after an injury.

Taking a person's hand, giving a hug, putting a hand on a person's shoulder or arm can mean a great deal to a person in emotional pain. Touching a person affirms dignity and self-worth.

A woman described her work as a nurse in a rehabilitation hospital for those who had experienced neck and head injuries. Some of her patients were paraplegic or quadriplegic. She said, "Just because a person has been injured doesn't mean that he has any less need to be touched or held. One of our patients is a twenty-seven-year-old woman who was injured in an automobile accident. Her husband and little girl drive more than forty miles one way, three times a week to visit her. Even though she can't feel anything from the neck down, and has very little control over her facial muscles, she somehow manages to kiss her little girl when her little girl leans over to hug and kiss her mother. She always has a much calmer demeanor after her husband gives her a long hug before he leaves. The sense of touch she has with them is her greatest link to the life she once knew."

So much is said today about unnatural or abusive forms of touching that many people have adopted an attitude, "Better not to touch at all than to be misunderstood or charged legally with a motive that wasn't intended." Even so, everybody I've talked to about touching knows intuitively when touching is good and welcome, and when it is bad and unwelcome. We all need "good touch." If you have a question about whether your touch will be welcomed by another person, ask the person. Don't make assumptions one way or the other. If you touch another person and that person pulls away or rejects your touch, don't force yourself upon the person.

If you have questions about what another person means or intends by touching you, ask the person. You may be reading into the touch a message that the person didn't intend. You can help the person become a better communicator by discussing the matter of physical touch. In the process, you might also become better informed about what others like and don't like about the way you relate to them physically.

Be sensitive to those around you who *need* an unsolicited show of your affection, concern, or compassion. Those who are grieving, who are in emotional pain, or who have just suffered a major disappointment or rejection nearly always appreciate a kind touch.

"But," you may say, "I wasn't raised to show affection in physical ways."

You may not have had a lot of experience in receiving or giving physical affection as a child. That doesn't mean you need to remain a cold, aloof person as an adult. You can change the way you relate to other people. Granted, it will take some courage for you to do so. It may take some practice. But if you choose to be a person who is warm and affectionate, you can become such a person. Ask God to help you show others how much you love them in ways that are appropriate and beneficial to you and the other person.

The key question to ask yourself is this: In giving my love and care to others, am I willing to touch them with the love of Christ?

3. Time

The loving father took time to listen to what his son had to say. Although we have no evidence that the father expected or required the confession his son made, the implication is that the father heard his son fully. Nothing else was as important to him in that hour as being with his son.

Furthermore, he immediately ordered that preparations begin for a celebration. Such celebrations in the culture at that time could last for days. The father made it clear he intended to spend some time with his son! He very well could have said to him, "Well, son, you get cleaned up for dinner, and we'll talk about this later." He could have said, "I've got lots of irons in the fire right now. I'll see you later when I have more time." He could have said, "Talk to my designated representative about getting together the things you need, and we'll touch base when the sun goes down." The loving father didn't take any of those approaches. He was present for his son when his son needed him most.

Our heavenly Father is available to us at all times. He is never too busy to hear our prayers. He is never preoccupied with other concerns to the point that He rejects our presence. Rather, He delights in having close, intimate communion with us. Whenever we are willing to spend time with Him, He is willing to spend time with us.

Some months ago I was feeling overwhelmed by some of the problems I was facing in my life, and I was feeling particularly lonely one night. I began to pour out my heart to God, telling Him how I felt and how miserable I was. Suddenly, it seemed as if the Lord Himself was standing at the end of the sofa on which I was sitting. I didn't see a vision of Him, but I had a very strong awareness of His presence. His presence was tangible to me, although unseen—a presence and power so strong that I really can't describe it accurately. I had no doubt He was there. Then it was as if the Lord spoke to my heart as He stood in my living room, conveying to me His message without any spoken words, *You have Me. Am I not enough for you?*

I responded, "Yes, Lord, You are." And I began to weep.

No matter how you may feel. No matter how you may have been rejected by others. No matter how much you may hurt or how lonely you may feel, you *always* have the Lord. He is all-sufficient.

Who could love you more than the Lord does?

Who other than the Lord can be there at all times for you?

Who can possibly understand you better or know more clearly exactly what you are feeling and what you need?

Who is better able to meet your needs and satisfy your longings?

Who other than the Lord is instantly with you the very moment that you call upon Him?

The Lord loves you with His presence. He is with you every moment of your life and for all eternity.

In giving your love and care to others, take time to listen to people—really listen. Hear them out. Don't cut them short. Let them tell you their whole story.

Take time to sit with those who are grieving or who have suffered loss or who are in the process of recovery. You don't need to say anything. Just be present.

A woman who was in a very serious accident said to me after her recovery, "There were times when I didn't know if I was going to make it, but then I'd turn my head and see that my daughter was sitting in the chair next to my bed. She might be knitting, reading, or even napping. She didn't have to say anything, and neither did I. Just her being there was all that needed to be said. I believe the hours my daughter spent by my bedside were just as important to my healing as the treatment and medications that the doctors and nurses gave to me. She gave me the most precious gift she could ever have given. She gave me her time."

Take time to show up at your child's game, recital, performance, or awards ceremony. Take time to play with your child and share meals with your child. Be there for your spouse when your presence is the best gift you can give. Sometimes a weekend away or a vacation is the greatest expression of love you can make. It says, "I just want to spend time with you."

Are you willing today to show your love in terms of time?

4. Gifts

The loving father gave gifts to his son upon his return: sandals, a ring, and a robe. Each was a special sign that the son was being restored to full family membership. Servants went barefoot. Sons wore sandals. Servants didn't own or wear jewelry. Sons could conduct family business with a family signet ring. Servants wore tunics only. Sons wore robes, including in many families, ones that were finely embroidered and that were considered to be family heirlooms.

The heavenly Father gives good gifts: "Every good gift and every perfect gift is from above, and comes down from the Father of lights, with whom there is no variation or shadow of turning" (James 1:17 NKJV). God's motives in giving to you are never shadowy and never manipulative. His motive is always unconditional love. He gives you life itself. He meets your material needs. He gives you challenges, opportunities, and work to do. He puts you into a family and gives you people to love and be loved by. He redeems you from evil and calls you His own.

He gives you free will to choose to serve Him and freedom in your spirit to be totally yourself in His presence. He gives you the beauty of nature. He allows you to own works of art and to decorate your home with possessions whose sole purpose is beauty. Every thing you can imagine as being good comes from God.

I knew as a boy what it meant to live with a person who gave me nothing. No compliments, no kind words, no tangible presents— I don't recall my stepfather ever giving me anything that could have been considered a gift of any kind. It would have been very difficult for anyone to convince me as a boy that my stepfather loved me. If you love others, you give to them.

Your gifts don't need to be expensive; in fact, they don't need to cost anything. They need to be gifts that come from the heart and show that you took the time and interest to give something that was appropriate and that you thought would be appreciated.

A little girl handed her mother a bright red-and-orange leaf that she had picked up from the yard. "It's a present to remind you that I love you," she said as her mother prepared to leave for work. "I looked through all the leaves that fell last night, and this one is the prettiest." Now, you can't tell me that wasn't a highly valuable gift! It was truly a gift from the heart, and it didn't cost a dime.

Love is giving. Your acceptance, touch, and time are gifts. So are words of encouragement and acts of service. But in a very important way, your tangible gifts are important expressions that you care enough to recognize a need or desire in the other person's life and are doing what you can to meet it.

A coat given to a person who is cold, a casserole given to a family in need or in grief, a bouquet of flowers from your garden to brighten the room of a person unable to leave the house, a telephone call to a friend far from home, a bill paid secretly for a person who is struggling to make ends meet, a card sent to a person who is lonely—all are gifts that convey love.

Do you care enough to give a gift today?

5. Words of Encouragement

Perhaps the greatest word of encouragement that the loving father gave to his son upon his return was: "son." He defined their relationship in terms that must have been highly encouraging to the boy. The father said, "This my son was dead and is alive again; he was lost and is found." The father called his boy alive and found. What comforting and wonderful music to his ears! He had a place, a role, a future, a position. He was wanted.

Your heavenly Father always speaks words of encouragement to you—He tells you that you are His child, His delight, His beloved one.

Your heavenly Father also believes that you can accomplish what He calls you to do. He trusts you to use the abilities He has given you.

Jesus told numerous parables and gave many teachings in which He expressed His belief that those who followed Him were capable of living in right relationship with God. He believed they could invest their God-given talents and multiply them. He believed they could withstand temptation, could discern evil from good, and could understand and apply the Word of God to their lives.

Your heavenly Father believes in you more than *you* believe in yourself. He calls you His child. He believes you are worthy and valuable beyond measure.

Are you willing to put your love into words of encouragement today?

6. Acts of Service

The loving father called for a celebration in honor of his son's return. He ordered the killing of the fatted calf—a calf that very likely had been fed for quite some time in anticipation of that very celebration. He said, "Let us eat and be merry." The celebration was complete with music and spontaneous, joyful dancing.

In what way was a party like that an act of service? The loving father was making a public statement to all in his community that he had fully and immediately accepted his son upon his return. There was no waiting period or proving time before the father publicly declared his full acceptance of his son *as his son*. The father's action was an act that reinstated his son's dignity and worthiness among the extended family and broader community.

Your heavenly Father extends to you the full privilege of being His child the moment that you turn to Him and receive His forgiveness. The person who accepted Christ sixty seconds ago is as much a Christian as the person who has loved and served Christ for the last seventy years.

Your heavenly Father continually helps you, prepares opportunities for you, gives you wisdom to make right choices, and strengthens you with courage. Each is an act of service to you.

Your acts of service to others may take any number of forms:

- Raking a sick neighbor's leaves.
- Dropping off a mother's children at school on a morning when she has a doctor's appointment.
- Doing a chore for a sibling so he can take part in a special event.
- Helping out around the house when you know Mom is tired.

- Baby-sitting for free so a couple with triplets can go out on a date.
- Bringing Dad his slippers when he collapses into an easy chair after a hard day at work.

To truly serve means to anticipate a need and then act to fill it without being asked.

Service can mean volunteering to help in simple ways—answering phones, delivering packages or meals, ladling soup, gathering cans of food, sewing buttons onto used garments, ironing linens used for a church function, manning a booth, helping an adult learn to read, or fixing a sandwich for a hungry child.

Service can also be prayer. Are you willing to take time to visit a person and pray with him or her about a need? Are you willing to intercede on behalf of that person until God answers your prayer?

Are you willing to give legs and arms—energy, effort, and talent—to your love?

Service Even After Failure

God isn't through with you yet! You may have failed at something in your life. You may have given in to temptation. You may have experienced a divorce. You may have failed in your business or suffered a major setback in your career. You may not have done the things as a parent that you now know you should have done. You may not have obeyed God in the past, and you failed to do what you believed He called you to do.

Those feelings can lead a person to conclude, "God has given up on me." I once heard a woman say, "I feel as if God put me on a shelf and He hasn't even dusted me for a long time."

Let me assure you today, if you are breathing, God is working in you, and He is desiring to work through you.

His love for you hasn't changed one bit. Even if you don't feel His presence or love as you perhaps once did, He still loves you just as much as He ever did or ever will. His love for you has no bounds, no beginning or ending.

Let me also assure you that He still has a great plan and purpose for your life.

Have you ever tried to tell something to someone and he didn't seem to understand you, no matter how many different ways you tried to tell him? It's as if he had a blockage of some kind. That same thing can happen in your relationship with God. If you have no prior relationship with Him, if you have a faulty understanding of Him, or if you have a wrong attitude toward God, you aren't going to hear what the Lord wants to say to you. The fault is not His. It's yours.

My purpose is not to blame you or lay some kind of guilt trip on you about this. Rather, I want to point out to you that we sometimes believe that God is finished with us because we have been taught incorrectly in the past or we don't understand how God works. At times, we don't want to believe that He has more for us to do.

Much of what you believe God desires for you to do is based upon what you have come to believe about God through the years. What is your understanding of God today?

Do you see God as a loving father or a demanding judge?

Do you see God as an intimate friend or a distant acquaintance?

Do you see God as a patient and gentle teacher or an intolerant and angry guide?

Do you see God as a faithful companion or someone who comes and goes from your life?

Do you see Him as a generous provider or a stingy God who reluctantly metes out His blessings?

Do you see God as understanding you thoroughly and yet loving you completely, or do you see Him as removed and conditional in His acceptance of you?

The way you regard God will determine to a great extent what you believe God desires to do in your life.

Disqualification

Others believe that they have sinned in a certain area, and because of that sin, God can no longer use them. That is *not* the gospel of Jesus Christ.

While it is true that God will not use a person who remains or willfully chooses to abide in sin, it is equally true that God always desires to use a person who abides in Him and His forgiveness and who chooses *not* to sin.

Moses killed an Egyptian, but God made him the leader of the people of Israel.

Abraham and Sarah erred in Abraham's fathering of a child by Hagar, but God called Abraham His "friend" and rewarded his faith by giving a son to Sarah.

David once pretended to be a madman, deceiving a king who had given him refuge, but God made him king over Israel.

Jacob tricked his father, his brother, and his father-in-law, but God made him the father of the twelve tribes of Israel.

Mary Magdalene was once filled with demons, but Jesus trusted her to tell His disciples about His resurrection.

Saul was a vicious persecutor of the church, even consenting to the death of Stephen, yet God used him as the apostle Paul to take the gospel to the Gentiles.

The difference in these people's lives was this: when they had an encounter with God, they said yes to Him. They were willing to turn from doing things their way to doing things His way. They didn't remain the people they once were. They chose instead to order their lives after God and to follow His plan for them.

As long as you are in sin, your sin disqualifies you from being a leader in God's kingdom. If you were the commander in chief of an army, you wouldn't put a known spy and traitor in charge of a division of your troops. If you were the head of a company, you wouldn't knowingly put an acknowledged thief and embezzler in charge of all your company funds. If you are serving Satan, God can't make you responsible for completing a task that is intended to benefit His kingdom.

Qualification Through Forgiveness

As much as sin disqualifies you, God's forgiveness qualifies you. There is only one unforgivable sin, and it doesn't apply to any person who still acknowledges that God is God. As long as you have any desire for God, you haven't committed the unforgivable sin.

The unforgivable sin is the sin of saying, "I don't need forgiveness. I don't need God. I don't want anything to do with God's love." As long as a person holds that position, God will not override the free will. He will not demand that the person love Him or receive His forgiveness. He will allow that person to remain in the sin because that is a willful choice. Therefore, a person with that attitude cannot be forgiven or saved from the sinful state. It has nothing to do with God's desire for that person. It has to do solely with the person's lack of desire for God.

If you have any desire whatsoever to know God or to receive God's wondrous love, or if you have ever accepted Jesus as your Savior, you have not committed an unpardonable sin.

Of course, some people set up false standards for behavior—standards that far exceed what the Bible requires. Jesus had trouble with such people in His day. The Pharisees insisted that a person follow every minute detail of the law in order to be considered righteous. The law they insisted be followed was a law largely of human creation—it was a law that went far beyond the Law of Moses in its detail and restrictions.

For example, the Law of Moses stated,

Remember the Sabbath day, to keep it holy. Six days you shall labor and do all your work, but the seventh day is the Sabbath

of the LORD your God. In it you shall do no work: you, nor
your son, nor your daughter, nor your male servant, nor your
female servant, nor your cattle, nor your stranger who is within
your gates. (Ex. 20:8–10 NKJV)

The law that the Pharisees followed went far beyond this. Their
law had dozens and dozens of restrictions about what specific activities could be done on the Sabbath and which were considered to
be illegal. According to their code, Jesus couldn't heal on the Sabbath.

Jesus' response to those who attempted to supersede the law
of God with their own laws was this:

They bind heavy burdens, hard to bear, and lay them on men's
shoulders; but they themselves will not move them with one of
their fingers. . . . Woe to you, scribes and Pharisees, hypocrites!
For you shut up the kingdom of heaven against men; for you
neither go in yourselves, nor do you allow those who are enter-
ing to go in. (Matt. 23:4, 13 NKJV)

The message of God's Word is one of forgiveness and mercy.
He freely and completely forgives, and He calls upon us to do
the same for one another. Whenever God forgives, we must forgive.

The apostle Paul made a clear distinction between those who
choose to remain in sin and those who have accepted God's forgiveness:

Do you not know that the unrighteous will not inherit the king-
dom of God? Do not be deceived. Neither fornicators, nor idol-
aters, nor adulterers, nor homosexuals, nor sodomites, nor thieves,
nor covetous, nor drunkards, nor revilers, nor extortioners will
inherit the kingdom of God. And such were some of you. But
you were washed, but you were sanctified, but you were justi-
fied in the name of the Lord Jesus and by the Spirit of our God.
(1 Cor. 6:9–11 NKJV)

Note that phrase "and such were some of you." Paul stated that there were those in the Corinthian church, whom he addressed as "those who are sanctified in Christ Jesus, called to be saints" (1 Cor. 1:2 NKJV), who once engaged in the most vile sins. *And yet,* God forgave them when they turned to Him. They didn't remain in their disobedience or unrighteousness. They received the righteousness of Christ in their lives. And God then used them to be His witnesses in the city of Corinth.

God's forgiveness of you qualifies you not only to be in eternal relationship with Him, but also to offer service *now.*

Love Is in the Giving—Even If There Is No Receiving

Your willingness to love must never depend upon another person's ability to give love back to you. Some people will never be satisfied with what you do for them. Some people will never feel worthy, no matter how much you encourage them or attempt to include them fully in your life. In risking love, you are also risking the possibility of being rejected or turned away. A person may even reject you while saying that he loves you!

The goal in loving is not to succeed in evoking the response you want from another person, but to do what you believe the Lord is pleased for you to do.

You must seek to give love in ways that others can accept your love, but if they cannot accept your love in spite of your best efforts, then you must ask yourself, Is God asking me to show love to this person? If so, then you can be assured that He accepts your efforts and values them. He will reward you by sending you someone who can receive your love, and who can return love to you in precisely the ways and in exactly the moments you need it most.

Also ask yourself, Can I accept the forms of love that others are showing to me? Be open to receiving the love of others.

Because your challenge as a Christian is to love others *even if they don't love you back*, you are never without somebody to love. Reciprocity is not required for this kind of love. The only thing that is required is your willingness, your desire, your commitment to open up and give to others something of who you are and what you have.

If you don't have somebody who needs you today or who counts on your love, find somebody! You only need to open your eyes and look around, and you'll find dozens of people within immediate range who greatly need to know that somebody cares for them.

Volunteer your time to an organization or group that needs an extra pair of hands or perhaps a particular skill that you have.

Join a group that shares your interests. Do so not with an eye toward what you can get from the group, but with an intent to give something to the group. Your gift of love may be baking cookies for refreshment time once a quarter, typing up minutes of the group meetings, offering your living room for meetings, or picking up members who no longer drive so they might attend the group's meetings.

Get involved with a church group actively engaged in ministry to others. It may be a group of ushers who assist with church services. It may be a group that goes door-to-door to deliver information about the church. It may be a group that prepares boxes of clothing and bedding to send to mission stations.

You'll find more opportunities to give than you ever dreamed possible. You'll find more people in need of love and compassionate care than you ever anticipated.

The Link Between Love and Hope

To love others is the greatest purpose you can know.

When you know that someone is counting on your help, when you know that you're making a difference in someone else's life, when you can see that your gifts of time and talent are greatly valued, when your loving touches are accepted and returned, when your words of encouragement fall on appreciative ears, and when your acceptance of another person creates a friendship or establishes a good relationship, you automatically have a sense of purpose and meaning for your life. You have a desire to love more, to give more, to extend yourself further.

And in that, there is hope. You want tomorrow to dawn because there is still a lot of loving that you have to do tomorrow. You want next week to roll around because there's still a lot of giving that you want to do next week.

On the other hand, if you isolate yourself and turn inward, refusing to acknowledge the hands that are reaching out to you and refusing to believe the encouragement that others attempt to offer, you will become increasingly depressed and have a growing feeling that you are worth nothing and that life is over.

Loving others is the most hope-filled thing you can do:

I have hope because I have people who need me to love them and give to them.

CHAPTER 7

GOD DESIRES TO FULFILL YOUR POTENTIAL

Recently, a man came to see me about a particular project, and in the course of our conversation, I asked him what new thing the Lord was doing in his life.

He replied, "What do you mean, what 'new' thing?"

I said, "Well, in my experience, the Lord is always doing something new in me. He is always working at some area of my life to sand away the rough edges and make me even more useful in the work that He has called me to do. Not only that, but He always seems to have some new challenge for me to undertake."

The man said, "I'm not sure God is doing anything new in me."

I said, "Do you have a sense that God is preparing you for something new in your life?"

"No," he said. "I think I'm doing what He wants me to do right now."

"That may be true," I said, "but I believe that God is preparing us for something even greater. In many ways I'm doing the same things I have done for years—preparing and preaching sermons, having an outreach ministry that is broadcast beyond my church, writing books, ministering to individual people whom God brings my way. But on the other hand, God has caused growth in each one of these areas. That's not only a growth in numbers and volume, but also a growth in depth. The Lord is leading me always into deeper waters. He's allowing me to minister more effectively and to preach with an even greater anointing."

The man just shook his head silently and then finally said, "I wish I could experience that. I guess I've just peaked at this level."

"I don't believe that," I said. "I don't think anyone ever gets to the end of potential. There's always more we can be. There's always more that God calls us to do and experience. We never stop growing."

"I agree with that, but right now, it just seems that God has put me on hold," he said. "Is there something I should do?"

"If I were in your shoes," I said, "and I felt that nothing was changing and nothing was growing, there are a couple of things I'd do.

"First, I'd ask God to show me *why* I'm not growing. I'd ask Him to reveal to me if there is something holding me back. There may be an area in your life that you need to face before you can move ahead."

"You mean like a sin?" he asked sincerely.

"It may be a sin that you haven't faced. It may be an area in which you have been wounded or hurt that God wants to heal before He calls you to a new challenge. It may be something else."

"Such as . . . ?" he asked.

"I believe there are times when God puts people on hold in their ministries because they are in rebellion. They are doing something *they* want to do rather than doing what God wants them to do. God won't allow them to succeed further in the area in which they are working or the relationship in which they are involved because He doesn't desire them to be in that career or relationship in the first place. God won't bless what God knows will destroy us or diminish us."

A thoughtful expression came to the man's face, and I could tell that the Holy Spirit probably was revealing to him what God desired to do in him even as I was speaking.

I said, "There are still other times when God calls us to a wilderness experience or what we perceive to be a dry time spiritually in order to test our obedience or to call us into a new and deeper relationship with Him. He may want us to spend more time in the Word or more time in prayer. He wants to draw us closer to Himself, and He strips away new challenges and opportunities and possibilities so that we might turn our full attention to Him and make Him not only our number one priority but also our sole priority."

"I think I have some soul-searching to do," the man said.

"There's one other thing," I said. "There are times when God has something for us to do, but we simply haven't asked Him to show it to us. We are so caught up in our busy lives that we haven't taken the time to seek Him and to ask Him to reveal what our next step should be. It's as if God is waiting for us to slow down enough so He can get a word in edgewise."

"You're right," he said thoughtfully. "I haven't asked God in a long time if there's something in my life that He wants to change, much less if there's something additional or something different that He wants me to do."

I assured him, "I believe that if you genuinely and sincerely ask God to show you what He has for you, and you ask Him to reveal to you anything that may be keeping you from being fully equipped and ready to undertake that challenge, He'll answer you. He *wants* you to grow."

I then invited him to take a look at these verses of Scripture with me:

> *I will run the course of Your commandments,*
> *For You shall enlarge my heart.* (Ps. 119:32 NKJV)
>
> *Enlarge the place of your tent,*
> *And let them stretch out the curtains of your dwellings;*

Do not spare;
Lengthen your cords,
And strengthen your stakes.
For you shall expand to the right and to the left,
And your descendants will inherit the nations,
And make the desolate cities inhabited. (Isa. 54:2–3 NKJV)

Your right hand has held me up,
Your gentleness has made me great.
You enlarged my path under me. (Ps. 18:35–36 NKJV)

I said, "God has an enlargement plan for you. He wants to expand you on the inside so He can expand your influence on the outside."

He smiled and replied, "I can see that I've got some growing to do."

God Has Given You a Great Potential

What I said to that man I know to be true in my life. One experience especially comes to mind.

Several years ago I went on a prayer retreat with those who have leadership positions at In Touch Ministries. We went away for a few days with no agenda other than to pray and to see what God wanted us to do during the coming year. Over the years, God has told us at times to continue what we were doing, perhaps with a modification or two. At other times, He has revealed a new direction that we were to take.

These retreat days are some of the most valuable days we spend each year. As we truly and humbly seek God—in prayer sessions that involve all of us as well as in individual times of prayer—God always reveals to us His plan. He may speak to me or one of the other leaders first, and then we experience a general confirmation that this is the direction God wants us to take. Sometimes He reveals His will to several of us at once during individual prayer times, and we are amazed at the oneness of purpose we feel when we come together to discuss what God has spoken to our hearts.

When each of us feels assured that God has shown us what He wants to accomplish in the coming months, we leave our retreat time with renewed enthusiasm, renewed focus, and a renewed drive to accomplish what God has called us to do.

During one such retreat, God spoke very strongly that He wanted us to take the gospel to every nation, every day. I asked a broadcast engineer who was present what that would involve. He explained the technology that was necessary, and as he spoke, there was a genuine unanimity among us that that was what the Holy Spirit was calling us to do. Our minds overflowed with ideas about how and when and where and whom to contact. Our hearts also overflowed with faith that God was calling us to undertake the project and that He was going to equip us fully for the task, including a provision of the necessary finances.

Sure enough, within weeks after the Lord revealed His will to us and we submitted our will to the accomplishment of His will, God began to provide the initial resources that we needed to enable the *In Touch* programs to be broadcast every day into every nation of the world—either through regular television frequencies or through radio or shortwave bands.

It was a genuine miracle to us. It was an expansion and enlargement of our ministry tent. But from God's perspective, it was simply the next step toward our accomplishing the collective potential that I believe He has for *In Touch,* as well as the next step toward the fulfillment of the individual potential for each one of us involved.

When God calls us to expand, He calls others around us to expand too. When He calls one person to grow, He is in the process of calling others who touch that person's life to grow also.

A Great Potential

The good news for each one of us is that God has given us a great potential. Our potential is vast—so much greater than most of us know. The majority of people never even stop to think about potential, and those who do usually estimate the potential as being much less than it actually is. As a result, we shortchange ourselves, achieve less, and fail to dream big enough dreams.

God is infinite, and when He pours Himself into us and into our abilities, we take on His capacity, not our capacity. When God pours Himself into the tasks that He calls us to do, there is no limit to how much He can multiply our efforts to accomplish His purposes.

Quality as Well as Quantity

Too often, I believe, we think of potential in terms of quantity only. We evaluate our growth and progress in terms of numbers.

As a preacher, I am quick to admit that we preachers are often as guilty of this as the next person. We define success in terms of the number of souls saved during a revival, the number of members in a church, the total dollar amount of a budget, the square feet of a facility, the net worth of a church plant. Certainly, those in the corporate world do the same, as do most people in their respective jobs.

The Lord gives us not only potential to grow in size, but also potential to grow in quality.

Perhaps the more worthy gauge for a pastor to use would be one to determine the spiritual depth of the members in his congregation, the extent of their love for God, the variety and effectiveness of their ministries to others, and the degree to which they are willing to extend themselves in outreach to the lost. God is not only after a vast number of souls added to His kingdom; He also desires those in His kingdom to grow in their depth of understanding of His Word, in their love for other people, and in their commitment to serving others as the Holy Spirit leads them.

When you think of your potential, don't limit yourself to thinking of ways in which you might expand your personal résumé to include more and greater accomplishments. Think in terms of spiritual depth. God has virtually unlimited growth for you in your inner person. He has boundless love for you and, therefore, a fullness of relationship with Him that only a few will experience—not because God desires to limit His availability, presence, or power to only a few, but because only a few will commit themselves to knowing God in more spiritually intimate ways.

The pursuit of quality should not be confused with perfectionism. Perfectionism is the attitude that everything must be done perfectly at all times in order to be acceptable. Perfectionism can be a trap. I have a tendency toward perfectionism, and I have to guard against it. The trouble with perfectionism is that nothing can ever be done so that it will continue to be perfect day after day, year after year.

A person can make herself miserable trying to be perfect and to do perfect work. Furthermore, the more a person is bound up in perfectionism, the more stress that person will feel about her performance, the more frustration she will feel at the lack of perfectionism she sees in herself and others, and the less she will accomplish because there will always be something more that could be added or done before a project is released.

The potential for quality that God calls you to pursue is a quality of relationships. God calls you always to a deeper relationship with Him—to a greater understanding of God's all-powerful, all-knowing, all-loving, and eternal nature. He calls you to learn more and more about how He does things so that you might follow His example. He calls you to greater intimacy with Him so that you can sense what God desires to see changed or accomplished on the earth. He desires that you be so close to Him that you can hear and feel His heartbeat for the lost.

This same potential for quality in relationships extends to those in your family and your circle of close friends. God desires for you to be so sensitive to people around you that you can sense when they are hurting without a word being spoken. He longs for you to be in relationship with other believers so that you might agree together with them in prayer and in ministry and, thus, accomplish more for His kingdom.

I encourage you to ask God to reveal the areas in which He desires for you to grow in your potential for quality relationships.

God Is Committed to Realizing Your Potential

Even though the world may not recognize your potential or help you achieve it, God does. He believes in you and advocates for you because He knows what He has put in you. He loves you because you are His child and for no other reason. He seeks to perfect you, however, because He knows the unique purpose for which He created you. God is never content with your having unrealized potential. He is relentless in seeking to help you bring your potential to full fruition.

God's process of perfection has two dimensions, like two sides of the same coin:

1. teaching and guiding
2. chastisement

You must embrace both processes.

The natural tendency is to like the teaching and guiding of the Holy Spirit, and to pull away from His chastising. Some have even gone so far in this era as to proclaim that every negative experience is from the devil, not God. That position cannot be supported by the Scriptures.

God always works for your ultimate and eternal good. From His perspective, all that He does is good and for good. But from your perspective, what God does is sometimes painful and difficult. You must be very cautious in concluding that something isn't good solely because it doesn't feel good to you.

Jim had a serious setback in his relationship with a young woman whom he had hoped to marry. He discovered that she had been secretly seeing another man. She said that she saw him because she wanted to be sure about her love for Jim. He gave her another chance, only to discover that she continued to see the other man under an even greater cloak of secrecy.

Jim's trust in her was shattered. Even so, he forgave her and tried to keep the relationship together. She eventually broke off the relationship. He blamed himself for not loving her enough, not being good enough for her. The pain he felt was intense. He had been deeply in love with the woman and had anticipated living in a happy marriage relationship with her. All of his hopes and dreams and plans seemed destroyed.

Initially, Jim blamed a number of people, including the devil, for the breakup of the relationship. I asked him, "Do you think perhaps it was God who caused this to come to light so that you might not marry her?"

He didn't respond, but I could tell by the look on his face that he didn't believe God had been involved in the painful experience. It was against his theology that God could have a part in anything that might feel negative.

I said to him, "I'd like to ask you four questions."

He said, "All right."

"First," I said, "do you truly believe that God loves you?"

He responded quickly, "I have no doubt that God loves me. Jesus is my Savior. God has rescued me from sin and has given me a new life. Yes, God loves me."

"Fine," I said. "Do you believe God knows about everything that happens to you?"

He again responded quickly, "Of course! He knows everything."

"Including what was happening between you and your girlfriend?"

"Yes," he said. "God knew about that too."

"Third," I continued, "could God have stopped this series of events if He had desired to stop them?"

He said a little more slowly this time, "Yes, He could have stopped what happened."

"But He didn't intervene," I said. "He *allowed* this to happen. And that brings me to the fourth question: Why did God allow this in your life?"

He didn't say anything, so I continued, "I believe there is something in this that God wants to teach you, refine in you, or change in you. Ask God what He desires to do in your life."

"But maybe all this has nothing to do with me. Instead, it's all about what God is doing in *her*. I'm not sure that I'm supposed to change as much as *she* should change."

"God will do something in her as well," I said. "He has her potential in mind as much as He has your potential in mind. But there's always something in every circumstance or situation that God uses to refine us."

As the weeks passed, Jim began to accept a new way of thinking. He came to the conclusion that God, indeed, had brought about the circumstances that led to his breakup with the woman. He came to see that God had spared him what no doubt would have been an even greater heartache had he married her. He also began to accept the fact that God was desiring to change some things in him about the way he related to women, about how he rather blindly entered into relationships and allowed his heart to rule over his spirit and head, and about how his relationships tended to be based upon lust more than spiritual values.

Jim later admitted to me, "I think perhaps God caused me to meet that woman and to be hurt by her so He could change some things in me and prepare me for the *right* woman when she comes along. I'm not the same guy I was, and that's good."

God uses a wide variety of methods to teach you and to chastise you in a way that will lead to change, growth, and refinement in your life. He is always seeking ways in which you might be perfected. The perfecting process may be difficult and painful, but in the end, if you submit to God's work in your life, it is always good. You may not like the way you feel as you are going through a period of chastisement, but you certainly will like the end result.

The Holy Spirit's Perfecting Method of Tutoring You

As I mentioned earlier, one of the processes that God uses in perfecting you is a "tutoring" process. In many ways, the Holy Spirit is your teacher, and the Word of God is the textbook from which He teaches.

Just as any good teacher, the Holy Spirit also from time to time gives you tests—not so that He might give you a grade, but so that you might discover the areas in which you still need to grow as well as appreciate how much you have grown in certain ways. The tests that God sends your way are never intended to destroy you. Neither are they for God's purposes of evaluation. He already knows your heart and what the outcome of the test will be. The test, rather, is for your sake. God wants you to know yourself better.

The apostle Paul painted a vivid word picture of this tutoring or guiding role of the Holy Spirit:

> *Now I say that the heir, as long as he is a child, does not differ at all from a slave, though he is master of all, but is under guardians and stewards until the time appointed by the father. Even so we, when we were children, were in bondage under the elements of the world. But when the fullness of the time had come, God sent forth His Son, born of a woman, born under the law, to redeem those who were under the law, that we might receive the adoption as sons. And because you are sons, God has sent forth the Spirit of His Son into your hearts, crying out, "Abba, Father!" Therefore you are no longer a slave but a son,*

and if a son, then an heir of God through Christ. (Gal. 4:1–7
NKJV)

Before you accepted Jesus Christ as your Savior and became a
Christian, you were under the tutelage of the law. The commandments
of God spoke to you just as a parent tells a two-year-old, "No, don't
touch that. Don't do that. Do this instead." The law provided a moral
boundary or fence for your life. The law was given to the children of
Israel not to make them good or to renew their souls, but to prepare
them for the Messiah and to keep them from the ravages of evil.

The law served, and continues to serve, as an X-ray machine or
a CT scanner for the inner person. These machines may help identify what is wrong with a person, but they don't cure a person. The
law might also be likened to a mirror. It helps a person identify what
may need to be "fixed," but it doesn't make a person beautiful.

Paul told the Romans that the foremost purpose of the law was
to lead a person to the recognition of sin and the need for a Savior:

*Now we know that whatever the law says, it says to those who
are under the law, that every mouth may be stopped, and all
the world may become guilty before God. Therefore by the deeds
of the law no flesh will be justified in His sight, for by the law
is the knowledge of sin.* (Rom. 3:19–20 NKJV)

The Holy Spirit applies the law to your heart. You experience
this as a sense of conviction, an awareness in your conscience of
right and wrong. The Holy Spirit will call to remembrance what the
Word of God says, or He will send people into your life who will
speak the Word of God to you either to remind or to teach you about
God's commandments. The Holy Spirit does this even before you
come to know Christ, and He continues to do this after you have
been saved. You never learn all of the textbook, even if you have read
the Bible dozens of times. You never outgrow your need for the Holy
Spirit as your tutor in teaching and explaining and applying the
Word of God.

Jesus said this about the Holy Spirit:

If you love Me, keep My commandments. And I will pray the Father, and He will give you another Helper, that He may abide with you forever—the Spirit of truth, whom the world cannot receive, because it neither sees Him nor knows Him; but you know Him, for He dwells with you and will be in you. (John 14:15–17 NKJV)

These things I have spoken to you while being present with you. But the Helper, the Holy Spirit, whom the Father will send in My name, He will teach you all things, and bring to your remembrance all things that I said to you. (John 14:25–26 NKJV)

Part of what the Holy Spirit does in your life is to remind you of the truth you have learned. Part of His role is to give you an understanding of what you have learned—He imparts to you God's reasons and purposes, and reveals to you God's deepest meanings and desires.

The law tells you that you have to. The grace of God as manifest in the Holy Spirit gives you the *want* to.

The law tells you that you must obey. The Holy Spirit has been imparted to you by the Father to help you obey.

The law tells you what must be done and not done. The Holy Spirit gives you the courage to obey.

The Holy Spirit has been given a number of descriptive names—the Spirit of Truth, the Counselor, the One Called Alongside to Help, the Helper. The Holy Spirit works in your life continually to nudge you, prompt you, and point you in the right direction.

God's Perfecting Method of Chastisement

In giving you free will, God gave you the freedom to fail, to make mistakes, to sin, and to fall short of your potential. Each of these is a different state, however. You may lump them together as if they are one, but they are not. The Holy Spirit operates in chastisement through each of these shortcomings in your life.

Failure

To fail is to fall short of a human-devised goal. Many people set goals that are unrealistic, and when they fail, they have a sense of being worthless. Others set goals but then never put them into a workable plan so they might pursue them effectively. Still others set goals but are too lazy to work at achieving them. When the goals aren't met, they have a sense of frustration and self-doubt.

You are wise to set goals for yourself only after you have prayed and asked God to help you set goals. There is nothing wrong with goals, but there is something wrong in driving yourself to achieve in areas that may not be the least bit important to God.

When you set goals that arise from prayer and the leading of the Holy Spirit, then God is your partner in helping you reach the goals. He won't lead you to set a goal that He doesn't intend for you to meet. He is present with you continually to show you His methods and to reveal His timing. When you fail, you must turn immediately to the Lord and ask, "Where did I miss what You had for me? Show me what to do." He'll reveal His plan if you will wait patiently and humbly in prayer before Him.

God, however, has no responsibility to help you reach goals that you have set for yourself without consulting Him. The Holy Spirit will allow you to fail when you engage in self-centered and self-engineered pursuits. You may feel this is a form of chastisement, but if you are truly honest with yourself, you must conclude, "God allowed me to fail. He gave me just enough rope so I could trip myself."

The Holy Spirit will allow you to fail in self-designed pursuits in order to bring you to a position where you seek *solely* to do what God wants you to do. That is His purpose in chastising you through failure. He longs for you to turn to Him first and ask, "What shall

I do? Where shall I go? What shall I say? Whom shall I call? Which choice should I make?" He wants you to be in a position of total reliance upon Him.

An associate of mine once counseled a woman who set a goal for herself of weighing 130 pounds. She was a large woman of Norwegian descent—nearly six feet tall, with a heavy bone structure. Weighing 130 pounds was a very unrealistic goal for her. She nearly starved herself into anorexia trying to reach that goal, which was not a goal that God had asked her to set. Furthermore, she spent a great deal of her time and energy in pursuit of her goal. Later, she admitted that she could have used that time and energy to much better advantage for the gospel's sake. When she finally accepted that 160 pounds was going to be a "thin" and healthy weight for her, she was free to explore the true potential that God had given to her spiritually, intellectually, and physically.

The Holy Spirit moves in to chastise you anytime you pursue goals that are contrary to God's purposes for you, and anytime you place your personal goals above God's goals.

Mistakes

Mistakes are innocent wrongdoings. In making a mistake, you have not willfully chosen to do wrong, although your actions may have terrible consequences or create difficult problems for you. This does not diminish the pain that you may experience in making a mistake.

A person walking in a blinding snowstorm may very innocently move too close to the edge of a cliff, lose his balance, and fall. When he falls, he discovers that the law of gravity pulls him toward a painful landing—even though he never intended to fall and certainly would have stayed far away from the edge of the cliff if he had known it was there. The same is true for many moral and ethical mistakes that people make in the course of their day-to-day lives. They do not intend to err, but they do.

The Holy Spirit sometimes intervenes sovereignly to keep a person from making a mistake, but if she chooses not to remain sensitive at all times to the leading of the Holy Spirit, she is subject to making routine mistakes that the Holy Spirit allows to be made. The divine purpose is ultimately one of chastisement—of allowing the person to learn from the pain of her errors.

A wise parent knows that at times a child needs to experience the painful consequences of error. Most of us tend to learn more effectively from what we do that is incorrect than from what we do that is correct. Certainly, a loving parent would not allow a child to experience permanent damage—emotional, physical, or spiritual—in allowing a child to make a mistake, but there are times when it is more effective to allow a child to reap what she sows, even if the harvest is painful.

I once met with a man who was suffering from intense grief after the death of his son. The man said to me, "I did everything for my son. I gave him everything I could think to give him. I was always there for him. I devoted my life to helping him. I did everything but allow him to experience failure."

The man's son became involved in crime—at first, petty offenses. The father was always there to bail him out and to make excuses for his behavior. He didn't punish him or deny him any privileges.

As the boy moved into his teenage years, he turned to using drugs and to running with a crowd of young people that had a very negative influence on his life. The father didn't intervene. When the boy was arrested for theft, the father provided the best lawyers that money could buy to get the boy probation.

What a shock the father experienced when his son was murdered a few years later in a drug deal that went sour. He said, "I thought I was loving my son by covering for his mistakes and not chastising him. I realize now that I would have loved my son better by saying no to him and by insisting that he abide by my rules and the rules of society. I raised a lawless child, and in the end, he was a victim of lawlessness."

The Holy Spirit allows you to make mistakes so that you might learn from them and, ultimately, so that you might rely totally upon the Holy Spirit to guide you in your day-to-day decisions and activities. Again, His purpose in chastisement is to bring you to a place of complete trust in God and God alone.

Sin

A sin is a breach in the relationship between you and God. A sin separates from God—it is a willful act of disobedience against God's commandments. The key word is *willful*. You sin if you engage in a behavior that you know is wrong; you deliberately act in a way that is contrary to God's Word.

The Holy Spirit certainly uses chastisement in bringing you to a confrontation with your sinfulness. He will prick your conscience with an ever-sharp needle until you acknowledge that what you are doing is wrong before God.

A woman once admitted to me that she shoplifted an item from a department store. She knew it was wrong to shoplift. She had been a Christian for several years, and she said, "I think I did it primarily as a lark, just to see if I could get away with it. It wasn't even an item I particularly wanted. I just wanted to see what it was like to do this." She made it out of the store with the item and at first, felt a rush of adrenaline that she had managed to steal and get away with it.

"Then," she said, "the Holy Spirit moved in on my case. Everywhere I turned, I saw that item. I'd open a drawer and it would be there. I'd open my purse and it would be there. I'd turn on the television set and I'd see a commercial for the item I had taken. I'd open a magazine and there it would be. I even started dreaming about the item. After several days of this, I couldn't wait to get back to the store to return the item. I managed to get it back on the shelf from which I had taken it without anybody noticing. I never felt such relief in my life. I asked God to forgive me and to help me never to give in to that kind of temptation again."

The Holy Spirit has no tolerance for continued sin in your life. He will convict you repeatedly and with increasing fervor so that you might turn from your sin and enter into the righteousness that God desires for you. He will allow you to suffer under the consequences of your sin until you repent of your ways.

Falling Short of Potential

To fall short of your potential is to fall short of what God has set as a destiny for your life. It is to fail to recognize what God has created you to be and do, or to recognize it and refuse to do it—through neglect, lack of effort, or outright rebellion.

The Holy Spirit continually compels you to move forward in your faith and in your spiritual growth. He is never satisfied with some human-created definition of status quo. He always seeks to bring you to the full perfection of Jesus Christ.

Therefore, when the Holy Spirit sees you steering away from God's divine purposes for your life, or sees you holding back or neglecting to put forth effort to do what God desires for you to do and be, the Holy Spirit will move to prod you to action. Often this takes the form of chastisement.

We may experience failure in the area of our lives that we are substituting for God's plan. I've seen this happen on several occasions.

I know one minister who realized when he was in his twenties that God was calling him to preach the gospel and be the pastor of a church. He rationalized away that call of God by saying, "I'll go into business, build myself a big nest egg, and then find ways to minister the gospel. That way, I won't need to rely on other people for my financial support. I'll be able to pay my own way and do more." Through the years, he continued to feel the Holy Spirit calling him to be a pastor, but he justified his behavior by saying, "I'm still building my nest egg. I'm teaching a Sunday school class and going on short-term mission trips. Plus, I'm supporting pastors and missionaries right now with my tithe, which is a much bigger tithe than I would be making if I was in full-time ministry."

The day came when the man's business career collapsed. His company downsized him right out of a job. Although he tried repeatedly for more than a year to find work, he discovered that other companies were downsizing as well, and those that were hiring were hiring people who were younger and for whom they had to pay a lower salary. He used up his nest egg in maintaining his standard of living during that year while he hunted for work. All the while, he felt the Holy Spirit continuing to call him to preach and to pastor.

Finally, he submitted to what God had intended for his life all along. He used the small amount remaining in his nest egg to go to seminary, something his wife was willing for him to do. In fact, his wife had always been willing for him to enter the ministry full-time. They lived very modestly during the years he was in seminary, and then he accepted the pastorate of a small church. They moved to a rural area and lived in a small parsonage.

In many ways, their new life had little resemblance to their former life, which had been marked by a large home, fancy parties, big cars, and expensive vacations. As a pastor, he lived in a small house, drove a moderate-sized car, and had very few vacation days—which he and his wife usually spent at a friend's mountain home. The parties they gave were small gatherings, mostly potluck dinners with parishioners. From the world's standpoint, they had taken a giant step backward.

However, from God's perspective, and from their perspective, they had taken a giant step forward.

You've never met a happier man and woman. They work long hours every day calling on their parishioners, visiting the sick, and engaging in the work of the church. He spends considerable time each day in prayer and in preparation of his sermons. She works with the women in the church, leading a weekly Bible study and helping with various missions projects. Their priorities have changed greatly. They spend very little on entertainment or possessions, but are content with what they do have. They've found that they are actually able to save more on their low salary as pastors than they ever did on his high salary in the business world. They have finally accepted God's destiny for their lives, and they are experiencing more fulfillment and a deeper sense of personal satisfaction than they have ever felt.

This man has said, "I'm no longer running from God. I'm running with God. The Holy Spirit no longer has to prod me to accept God's will. Rather, He and I have a daily conversation about how I can best do God's will in this community of believers."

The Holy Spirit works in the life of every believer to get that person to the position of accepting and doing what God desires. The foremost desire of God, of course, is that we trust Him with the entire heart, mind, and soul. Anything that we trust more than we trust God is something that the Holy Spirit will actively seek to remove from our lives.

Why? Because the thing that we trust more than God has become an idol in our lives. God will not allow His children to worship anything or anyone other than Himself. He does this out of His love for us. He knows that if we worship anything or anyone other than Him, we are following a path that will lead to heartache. He longs to spare us the pain of deception, destruction, and death.

Anything that we place into a position of greater priority than God is something the Holy Spirit will seek to remove from our lives.

I have known countless people who had financial or career reverses primarily because they had come to trust their wealth more than they trusted God. They had placed a greater priority on their financial statement than on their relationship with their heavenly Father.

I have known people who experienced failures in relationships or setbacks in their health, who later admitted that they knew God was seeking to draw them closer to Himself and to trust Him more.

These acts of chastisement are not acts that God metes out in anger or hatred. No! They are acts of His love for us, to bring us to the place where we are willing to submit the entire self—including potential—to Him.

A Submitted Will, Not a Broken Spirit

God desires to bring you to a place where you are willing to submit to Him every aspect of your life—your marriage, friendships, business and business relationships, ideas, feelings, desires and ambitions, goals and dreams, ministry, opportunities. Everything! He moves against anything that keeps you from total submission to Him and total reliance upon Him. His purpose in chastising you is not to break your spirit, but to bring you to the place where you will submit your will.

I love to get out into the backcountry of the Rocky Mountains. The best way into the wilderness is usually by horseback. I have ridden a number of horses that seemed to sense what I desired with just a small tug on the rein, a shift in the saddle, or a softly spoken word. The horses were well trained and completely broken. They were in total submission to their riders.

The horses were not, however, without spirit. They were lively and energetic, and if given the freedom to run, they willingly took off at a gallop. They were high-spirited, but broken in will.

On the other hand, I've had a couple of horses that were impossible. They didn't do what I wanted them to do no matter how hard I pulled on the reins or prodded them with the stirrups, or how loudly I spoke to them. Believe me, they were no pleasure to ride. They supposedly were broken, but they certainly were not very well broken in my opinion. They were stubborn old nags, but not necessarily horses with lively spirits.

The Holy Spirit's desire is to bring your will to submission, not to break your spirit. The person with a broken spirit lacks energy, enthusiasm, and vision—a person who languishes in apathy and despair. The person with a broken spirit is one likely to rebel against God by putting his feet into the wet cement of stubbornness. Such a person is of little value to the gospel!

God's desire is not to destroy us, but to mold us, perfect us, and refine us so He can use us. Perhaps in no other Bible story do we see this more clearly than in the story of Jonah. (See Jonah 1:2.)

God set before Jonah his destiny, his purpose for being, his reason for living—go to Nineveh, capital of the Assyrian Empire, and preach God's Word.

When Jonah rebelled against this call of God and chose instead to board a ship bound for Tarshish, a place in the opposite direction of Nineveh, Jonah was turning his back on God's potential for his life.

God certainly could have killed Jonah at any time if His desire had been to destroy Jonah. God could have allowed him to fall from his donkey on the way to Joppa where he boarded the ship. He could have caused him to go down in the storm that nearly capsized the ship. He could have allowed him to drown in the wind-tossed waters. Instead, God used the various circumstances—ones that brought Jonah right to the doorway of death—to bring Jonah to a place of submission and compliance to God's plan.

All along, the Scriptures tell us that God

- "sent out a great wind on the sea" (Jonah 1:4 NKJV).
- "prepared a great fish to swallow Jonah" (Jonah 1:17 NKJV).
- "spoke to the fish, and it vomited Jonah onto dry land" (Jonah 2:10 NKJV).

God was in control of the situation at all times. He was chastising Jonah, bringing him to the place where Jonah would say,

I will sacrifice to You
With the voice of thanksgiving;

I will pay what I have vowed.
Salvation is of the LORD. (Jonah 2:9 NKJV)

The Holy Spirit will continue to work in your life until you come to that same place—a place of saying to God, "Not my will, but Yours. My life is in Your hands. Whatever You want me to say, I'll say it. Whatever You want me to do, I'll do it. Whatever You want me to be, I'll be it."

Always bear in mind that a person with a submitted will can still have a lively spirit. Such a person retains an eagerness and an enthusiasm for doing God's will—a desire that often translates into a focus of energy and an ability to endure that enable great mountains to be moved for the sake of God's kingdom. It is not the spirit that is broken, but the will that has been submitted.

The Holy Spirit not only woos you toward God's plan for your life, but He chastises you when you fall away from God's plan. He hedges you in, even as He calls you forward.

God's purpose is rooted in love, not anger.

His methods are aimed at refining you, not destroying you.

His goal is one of your perfection, not your demise.

Healing and Your Potential

In bringing you toward the fulfillment of your potential, the Holy Spirit often acts as an agent of healing in your life. Both processes described earlier are usually at work in the healing process.

I heard about a physician who described his work as having a twofold nature. He said, "Part of my work is in cleaning out wounds. As a surgeon, I cut away diseased tissue and use numerous processes to rid the body of rampant infection. This is the *cleansing* part of my work as a doctor."

He then went on to say, "The second part of my work is in assisting the healing process. I apply balm to open wounds and then bandage them. I prescribe medications that will assist the body in fighting infection. I build an environment in which healing can occur. This is the *building* part of my work as a doctor. For the vast majority of my patients, both cleansing and building are necessary for the healing process to be completed."

The Holy Spirit often heals in the same two-step process. He uses chastisement to cut away the dead tissue that corrupts your relationship with God. Once you have submitted to this cleansing process, He then gives you the strength and courage to embrace your potential and to begin to live your life according to the fullness of God's plan for you, which always includes some form of ministry or outreach to others.

Jesus described this "cutting away" or "cleansing out" process as one of pruning: "Every branch in Me that does not bear fruit He takes away; and every branch that bears fruit He prunes, that it may bear more fruit" (John 15:2 NKJV).

The purpose of the cutting away process is that you might eventually be more fruitful. God has a ministry purpose in mind even as He applies the pruning knife to the area in your life that needs to be adjusted.

One area in which many people need healing is in the area of old memories and past hurts. They are living with diseased emotions that keep them from embracing their potential.

For example, a parent might have said repeatedly to a person when she was a young child, "You are never going to amount to anything." The child is likely to develop such low self-esteem and to place such a low value on her life that she has no awareness of having a great God-given potential. Before she can develop potential, she first must believe that she has one!

Parents and teachers sometimes spend all their time pointing out the failures and faults of children without praising their successes and achievements. Others link performance with love, causing children to grow up with a "works" orientation because the only love they know is conditional love based upon what they do.

The result is damage—unfruitful branches in a person's psyche, diseased emotions, or a weakness in knowing right from wrong.

The Holy Spirit, if allowed to do His healing work fully, will move into that person's life to say, "You are going to amount to something in God's kingdom. I'm going to help you achieve it." The Holy Spirit will arrange for people to come into the person's life to help him get beyond those early negative influences. In most cases, the person will need to forgive whoever hurt him in the past. The Holy Spirit calls him to do that, and even more, He enables him to do it.

The Holy Spirit applies a balm of unconditional love to your life. He will send people your way to show you that genuine love is not based upon what you do, but is extended solely on the basis of who you are as a child of God.

The Holy Spirit will send you people who will affirm your talents and abilities that God has placed in your life, and who will encourage you to use your abilities even though you may have temporary learning failures or setbacks as you grow. He will send you people who will be patient with you and encourage you in your relationship with God and your efforts to minister to other people.

The healing process is not necessarily an easy one, a short one, or one without pain. It sometimes involves opening up old wounds in order to recleanse them so they might heal completely. When you are experiencing the pain, you are likely to say to God, "Stop! I'd rather let bygones be bygones. Healing is too painful!"

God loves you too much, however, to allow you to live in an emotionally or spiritually sick state. He will press and prune and chip away at the rough calluses on your soul in His effort to cleanse you of old hurts and refine you emotionally until you experience the fullness of His healing power.

In recent years, there have been times when I felt as if God was putting me through the emotional wringer. Have you ever seen an old-fashioned washing machine that had a wringer on the top of it? In using a wringer, a person put a garment through two rollers, under pressure, so that as much water as possible might be squeezed out of a garment. Modern machines have a spin cycle that accomplishes the same purpose.

There have been times when I thought there was no way I could cry another tear. There have been times when I thought God had squeezed out of me all the hurt a person could possibly feel. And then, I discovered there were still more tears and still more degrees of pain to face.

Each time God revealed to me something new that I needed to confront, I did so with this prayer, "Holy Spirit, heal me. Cleanse me of this. Help me to come out of this situation stronger, not strangled. Help me to emerge from this better, not bitter. Help me to be free of any emotional baggage that might weigh me down and keep me from being all that You want me to be."

And each time, the Holy Spirit was faithful to be my Healer. He brought me through the pain so that I reached a place of having greater and greater freedom to be myself, to express myself, and to do what God had called me to do. Bit by bit, month by month, experience by experience, adverse circumstance after adverse circumstance, He worked to turn what seemed to be negative into a giant positive. There were hard places in me that He softened, jagged edges that He smoothed, raw places that He covered gently, tough places that He made tender. I feel things today that I didn't feel before I submitted to the Holy Spirit's healing process that came in the wake of some very tough personal times. In my mind, I might have known *how* I should feel, but to actually have the feelings flowing freely inside was a new experience for me in many areas of my life. I know without a doubt that I have much greater compassion for and empathy with hurting people today than I had several years ago.

And that healing process continues. I'm increasingly willing to submit myself to the searching, searing light of the Holy Spirit because I know that even if the process is initially painful, the end result is joyous. I know that cleansing and a building-up process are at work that are for my good and for the good of those whose lives are touched by my ministry.

One person said to me not long ago, "Dr. Stanley, I used to admire your preaching a great deal, and I'm sure I learned much from you. But your preaching in the last few years has been so much deeper and richer and more directly related to my life that I am *grateful* you've gone through this hard time in your life. I'm one of the many who have benefited from your pain."

The person who said this to me is a friend, so my first response was to say wryly, "Glad to be of service." In my heart of hearts, however, I truly meant that. I *am* glad, and grateful to God, that I can be of greater service to people. That's what God desires for each of us: that we might make a greater and greater commitment to Him, and be cleansed and strengthened in the inner person to greater and greater degrees, so that we might be of greater and greater service to Him at deeper and deeper spiritual levels.

God's Healing of Your Misplaced Dependency

The Lord desires to heal you of old emotional and spiritual wounds and memories, and to heal you so completely that you no longer rely on any of the crutches you have used in the past as a substitute for trust in God.

When someone injures a knee, leg, or ankle, she may be given a pair of crutches so she can walk without putting her weight on the injured bones and tissues. This same thing happens to us when we are injured emotionally. We turn to various crutches in hopes that we can continue to live our lives without putting any stress on that area of pain.

These crutches take a variety of forms. Some people depend on a certain person or group of people to fill the gap left by a spouse who has abandoned them or a parent who has rejected them. They go beyond a normal or healthy reliance upon these people. Rather, they expect this person or group to be a substitute spouse or parent. They rely on them for decisions. They press them for love. They make demands upon them to support them in ways that only God can do. In essence, they have made other people a crutch, one that they continue to use long after they should have been healed of their emotional pain.

Other people turn to the crutches of alcohol, overuse of prescription drugs, or illegal drugs. They attempt to drown or mask their sorrow or emotional pain rather than devote their energy to getting well. Long after the painful experience, they still rely on the crutch.

Some people turn to counselors and therapists as long-term crutches. Now, I'm all for good Christian counseling. I've benefited greatly from those to whom I have turned for advice that is based upon God's Word and couched in prayer. But some people use their counselors as crutches to keep them from facing fully the truth of God's Word or the healing of the Holy Spirit. They prefer to remain moderately ill in their emotions rather than to face life squarely and rely on the Holy Spirit to heal them, strengthen them, and comfort them. They end up spending years, sometimes decades, with a counselor and have very little progress to show for their time and money.

Some people use their businesses or careers as crutches. Generally speaking, these people have experienced some type of financial setback in their lives. They might have lost a job, or perhaps they were raised in poverty. Rather than seek to recover from that situation and trust God fully, they hold back some of their trust and place it in their bank account, their job, their ability, their talent, or their connections to provide for them the resources they need. They are afraid to rely totally upon the Lord to meet their needs, afraid to place their full weight of faith upon Him, so they use a crutch of their own making. They end up using their work demands as a justification for going to the office on Sundays rather than to church. They point toward their fixed income or need to build a retirement plan as a reason for failing to give to God's work. They are relying on a financial crutch.

Some people use their parents or spouse as a crutch. They refuse to face their own lives. Rather, they blame a parent or spouse for everything that they perceive has gone wrong in their lives. They justify themselves completely and project their faults onto others.

Anything that a person uses as a substitute for total reliance upon and trust in God is a crutch.

The Holy Spirit has no tolerance for such crutches. If we fail to heed His call to trust in Him, and in Him alone, He will pull the crutches away from us in hopes that we will turn to Him and say, "I can't do anything without You. You are the Source of my entire life. You are the only One on whom I can *always* count."

You may be asking, "Dr. Stanley, are you saying that I shouldn't help other people with their problems?"

No, that's not what I'm saying. God calls us as Christians to help carry the burdens of others, but He does not call us to be crutches for others over an extended period of time. In the medical world, crutches are intended as a temporary stopgap measure; they are to be used only until the bones and tissues of the body have had time to heal. They assist a person from injuring himself further. The same is true for our role in the lives of those who have been hurt emotionally and physically. We are to be present to provide temporary strength and help until they have time to heal. We are to help them guard against situations and circumstances that might hurt them further.

A period of recovery is required from life's tragedies—whether it is the grieving period after the death of a loved one, the period during which a person must regain balance after a bankruptcy, or the period in which a person must rebuild her life after a devastating house fire or earthquake. We are to be there for others to help them carry their burdens and to protect them from further harm. We are not to be there, however, as a permanent solution in others' lives.

God alone wants to be the permanent—yes, eternal—solution for every difficulty or problem you encounter. The Lord makes it very clear in His Word that He desires for you to trust in Him alone for your total healing. He is the ultimate and final Source of your strength, healing, and comfort. God wants you to be utterly and completely dependent upon Him, not upon any other person or thing.

The Holy Spirit may chastise you to bring you to the point that you are willing to give up your crutches. When you do so and turn to Him, He is always there to catch you—to support you, undergird you, and impart to you His strength.

God Alone Can Give Fulfillment and Meaning

Many people believe that if they can reach a certain status, a certain income, a certain standard of living, a certain amount of fame, they will have fulfilled their potential, and they will experience happiness. They equate acquisition with satisfaction, and accomplishment with fulfillment.

They invariably discover that the acquisition of things, including position and status, does not necessarily result in satisfaction. In fact, the opposite is likely to be true. The person who has acquired a great deal always sees what more might be acquired. Having attained a quarter-carat diamond, she desires a two-carat diamond. Having purchased a Cadillac, he desires a Rolls Royce. Things don't satisfy. They only whet the appetite for further acquisition.

The same holds true for those who believe they will feel satisfaction if they are able to marry a certain person, live at a certain level of society, or have a home in the "right" neighborhood. They spend a lifetime trying to arrive and, upon arrival, discover they still long to be someplace else.

Neither does accomplishment result in fulfillment. A person might accomplish a great many things in life and have a personal résumé a dozen pages long, and still have a restlessness of spirit that says, "I need to do more."

The only genuine satisfaction and fulfillment that you will experience in life lie in this: accepting God's love, receiving God's forgiveness, and living in God's grace.

The person who accepts God's love experiences a deep-seated satisfaction that no matter what happens, God is present. The person who accepts God's love invariably must accept God's provision for forgiveness—Jesus Christ crucified and resurrected. That is the only means that God has provided for you truly to feel deep satisfaction that your spirit has been cleansed and renewed. Unless you know that you are forgiven, you cannot know the satisfaction of feeling safe from the assaults of the devil, the satisfaction of feeling free from the weight of guilt and sin, the satisfaction of knowing that God has provided an eternal home for you, or the satisfaction of knowing that God is the provider of unshakable security.

God's love and God's forgiveness go hand in hand. So do God's love and God's grace.

When you accept God's grace, you rest in the knowledge that God is in control of your life. You aren't the one in control. What happens to you is ultimately of God's doing. He is responsible for the consequences and the fashioning of your life. As He leads you from person to person, task to task—to say and do and be His person on the earth—you have an abiding sense that you are fulfilling His purpose for your life. That is the greatest feeling of fulfillment you can know. Such is a life of great meaning and purpose.

Anything that you try to engineer on your own will ultimately fail, crumble, or disappoint. When you trust God completely to define your potential and help you achieve it, you can relax and allow Him to arrange all things for your ultimate good, which in turn will be for the ultimate good of His kingdom. There is a rest that comes in knowing that God is in charge and that His grace is sufficient.

One of the most beloved hymns of all time is "Amazing Grace." I invite you to read through the words of all six verses of this hymn and to note the progression. The first two verses speak of God's grace in bringing us to the place of receiving God's forgiveness and love. The next two verses speak of God's grace in helping us to develop and use our potential. The final two verses tell of God's grace in preparing for us the place where our potential ultimately will be realized fully.

Amazing grace! how sweet the sound
That saved a wretch like me!
I once was lost, but now am found,
Was blind, but now I see.

'Twas grace that taught my heart to fear,
And grace my fears relieved;
How precious did that grace appear
The hour I first believed!

Through many dangers, toils, and snares,
I have already come;
'Tis grace hath brought me safe thus far,
And grace will lead me home.

The Lord has promised good to me,
His word my hope secures;
He will my shield and portion be
As long as life endures.

Yea, when this flesh and heart shall fail,
And mortal life shall cease,
I shall possess, within the veil,
A life of joy and peace.

When we've been there ten thousand years,
Bright shining as the sun,
We've no less days to sing God's praise
Than when we'd first begun.

God's grace truly is amazing. But it's the only thing that truly satisfies the longing for meaning and purpose in life.

When you truly grasp the fact that God, in His great love, has given you your potential and is committed to helping you fulfill your potential, you can't help having hope. When you only acknowledge that you have potential—a potential you haven't fulfilled—hope dissipates and is replaced by frustration and despair.

Rekindle your hope today by regaining sight of your God-given capacities as well as God's total commitment to helping you use your capacities to the maximum and to heal you so that you might experience genuine wholeness in your life—spirit, mind, and emotions.

I trust you can join with me in declaring today,

I have hope because God is the One who is in charge of fulfilling the potential He has given me.

CHAPTER 8

GOD HAS PROMISES YOU HAVEN'T EXPERIENCED YET

A young man walked down the aisle of our church recently, and to my surprise, he announced to me, "I just got out of prison." He had been in prison for several years and had actually anticipated spending a much longer time in prison. He had been paroled earlier than he expected.

He said, "When I went to prison, I thought my life had ended. I lost all hope." In his cell block, however, there was a television set, and he began to watch our *In Touch* program. At first he sneered and didn't pay much attention, but as the weeks went by, he became more interested. He said, "I kept hearing you talk about how God loves us and how God is good. I thought, *Well, if God is good, why am I in here? Why have so many bad things happened to me?* But week after week you kept telling me that God loved me. Finally, I said to myself,

Maybe this is true. I was so hopeless, I figured this was better than the way I was feeling. I didn't see anything I had to lose."

The young man began talking to another man in prison—a Christian—and the man led him to Christ. He said, "For the first time in my life, I began to think that I might have a future. I had never thought about having a future before. I never thought I could have one. But when Christ came into my life, I began to think in terms of my future." He then said that he wanted to join the church so he could soak up everything he could about God and what God might have for him to be and to do. He said, "I do believe that God can use me now."

God's Conditional Promises

Part of what God has for you to experience in your life—a part of your equipment for being who He wants you to be and doing what He wants you to do—are His many promises. Some of these are conditional promises, in which God says, "If you will do thus and so, I will do thus and so." You can keep yourself from receiving the fulfillment of God's conditional promises if you fail to do your part.

Other promises are ones that God says He is going to fulfill regardless of what you may do—these are the promises that relate to all of humanity or to His people as a whole. These promises were made possible by what Jesus did or according to what God has said. You cannot make them happen or keep them from happening.

Perhaps no place in the Bible are the conditional blessings of God spelled out in greater detail than in Deuteronomy 28–30. Read these words of potential blessing that God gave to His people:

> *Now it shall come to pass, if you diligently obey the voice of the LORD your God, to observe carefully all His commandments which I command you today, that the LORD your God will set you high above all nations of the earth. And all these blessings shall come upon you and overtake you, because you obey*

the voice of the LORD your God: Blessed shall you be in the city, and blessed shall you be in the country. Blessed shall be the fruit of your body, the produce of your ground and the increase of your herds, the increase of your cattle and the offspring of your flocks. Blessed shall be your basket and your kneading bowl. Blessed shall you be when you come in, and blessed shall you be when you go out. The LORD will cause your enemies who rise against you to be defeated before your face; they shall come out against you one way and flee before you seven ways. The LORD will command the blessing on you in your storehouses and in all to which you set your hand, and He will bless you in the land which the LORD your God is giving you. The LORD will establish you as a holy people to Himself, just as He has sworn to you, if you keep the commandments of the LORD your God and walk in His ways. Then all peoples of the earth shall see that you are called by the name of the LORD, and they shall be afraid of you. And the LORD will grant you plenty of goods, in the fruit of your body, in the increase of your livestock, and in the produce of your ground, in the land of which the LORD swore to your fathers to give you. The LORD will open to you His good treasure, the heavens, to give the rain to your land in its season, and to bless all the work of your hand. You shall lend to many nations, but you shall not borrow. And the LORD will make you the head and not the tail; you shall be above only, and not be beneath, if you heed the commandments of the LORD your God, which I command you today, and are careful to observe them. So you shall not turn aside from any of the words which I command you this day, to the right or the left, to go after other gods to serve them. (Deut. 28:1–14 NKJV)

Is there anything that a man or woman could desire that isn't covered in this conditional promise of God's blessing?

God tells His people that He will provide them with these things:

- Peace in both the city and the countryside (so that there will be no need for armed fortresses)

- Children who are a blessing
- Plenty of food and material goods
- Success in their work
- The accomplishment of everything they set their hands and minds to do
- Victory over their enemies
- An ongoing and lasting prosperity, not merely a temporary or seasonal one
- A firm relationship with God as His holy people
- An excellent reputation with other people
- The opportunity to be a blessing to others
- Leadership opportunities for the good of all

If you were to define what it means to be fulfilled in your life's work and to have all that truly matters in this life, you'd probably list these very things!

What do you need to do to avail yourself of this blessing?

- Diligently obey the voice of the Lord.
- Carefully observe all His commandments.
- Do not follow after other gods.

God went on in the following verses of Deuteronomy 28 to identify what would happen if His people did not obey Him or keep His commandments. Deuteronomy 28:20 (NKJV) summarizes the condition: "The LORD will send on you cursing, confusion, and rebuke in all that you set your hand to do, until you are destroyed and until you perish quickly."

We Must Do Our Part

I heard about a college professor who had a student complain that he had been unfair in giving the student a failing grade. The professor called for a conference with the young man and the chairman of his department to confront the student with the accusations that he was making against him.

The young man said, "Your course is too difficult. You expect too much of us students."

The teacher replied, "Out of forty students in your class, thirty-eight passed the course."

The young man sputtered, "Well, I think your tests are unfair. They aren't clear."

The professor asked, "How much did you study for each of the four tests in this course?"

The young man refused to reply but instead said, "You've had it in for me since the first day of class. You wouldn't answer my questions in class."

The professor said, "What was my frequent question to you when you asked questions in class?" The student sat in sullen silence. The professor said, "Didn't I ask you, 'Have you read the assignment in the text?'"

The professor then got out his class attendance book and said, "You were absent from class fourteen times out of fifty-one class and lab sessions. That's about 30 percent of the time. You failed eight out of ten multiple-choice quizzes that were directly related to textbook readings and that were graded by other students during class hours. I can't help concluding from those scores that you didn't read the text. You scored 40 percent on two of the exams and less than 30 percent on the other two."

The young man then asked belligerently, "Do you know who my father is? Do you know the size of the contributions he has made to this school and what is at stake if you fail me?"

The professor said, "I believe I would be failing to do the right thing by you if I gave you a passing grade."

The department chairman had heard enough at that point. He said, "This professor didn't give you a failing grade, young man. You earned a failing grade by what you didn't do. I'd be happy to have a conference with your father in attendance if that's what you want."

The young man stormed out of the professor's office in a rage.

Before you get mad at God for not blessing you enough, or become angry with Him for certain situations in your life, you need to ask yourself honestly, Have I been listening intently to what God has to say to me? Have I been reading His Word so I will know His commandments? Have I been heeding His commandments and observing them carefully in my life? Have I allowed myself to begin to worship idols—to hold some material possessions or relationships in my life with greater regard and devotion of time and service than I hold my relationship with God?

Many of God's promises of blessing are ones that are contingent on what you do or don't do.

Another of God's conditional promises to His children is found in Exodus:

> *If you diligently heed the voice of the LORD your God and do what is right in His sight, give ear to His commandments and keep all His statutes, I will put none of the diseases on you which I have brought on the Egyptians. For I am the LORD who heals you.* (15:26 NKJV)

Again, your part is to listen to God and keep His commandments to you. His part is to keep you free of the diseases of the Egyptians, which to a great extent were diseases caused by infected water, plants, and animals, as well as rampant sexually transmitted diseases.

God is a God of healing, but you must do your part.

A Lifestyle of Blessing

The Cross is God's designated entryway to a lifestyle of blessing. The Cross is the means by which you become God's person, a part of the greater family or people of God. A lifestyle of grace is something God desires for all of His children. It is a lifestyle marked by these qualities:

- Acceptance—God's acceptance of you and your acceptance of Christ
- Availability—of yourself to God and God to you
- Abundance—for total prosperity and wholeness
- Abiding—Christ in you and you in Christ so that you might bear much fruit
- Accountability—facing up to your faults and sins so that you might repent of them and thereby remove the obstacles that limit blessing

A Lifestyle Marked by Acceptance

The Cross assures you of God's acceptance. When you believe in Jesus, God considers all barriers between you and Him to be removed. Full reconciliation and intimacy of relationship are possible.

God's acceptance and forgiveness of you, and God's acceptance and blessing of you, are related to your acceptance of God. Accepting God's forgiveness is not a matter of works. It's a matter of opening your heart, mind, and hands to *receive*. There is no earning or striving involved.

I want you to read me very closely on this point because the promises related to God's blessing are very closely tied to this matter of acceptance.

Many people question whether they can ever be accepted by God. They say, "I've committed too many sins," or "I've committed a sin that is too big," or "I've sinned after God forgave me, so how could He forgive me again?"

The Cross is God's plan to assure you that you can never sin too many times or commit a sin that's too big or too terrible. You simply cannot "outsin" God's desire and ability to forgive you.

Later in Deuteronomy we read these words,

Now it shall come to pass, when all these things come upon you, the blessing and the curse which I have set before you, and you call them to mind among all the nations where the LORD your God drives you, and you return to the LORD your God and obey His voice, according to all that I command you today, you and your children, with all your heart and with all your soul, that the LORD your God will bring you back from captivity, and have compassion on you, and gather you again from all the nations where the LORD your God has scattered you. If any of you are driven out to the farthest parts under heaven, from there the LORD your God will gather you, and from there He will bring you. Then the LORD your God will bring you to the land which your fathers possessed, and you shall possess it. He will prosper you and multiply you more than your fathers. And the LORD your God will circumcise your heart and the heart of your descendants, to love the LORD your God with all your heart and with all your soul, that you may live. (Deut. 30:1–6 NKJV)

God told His people that even if they disobeyed Him and suffered the consequences of being scattered to the ends of the earth, if they repented—turned their hearts back to Him and followed what He commanded them—He would restore them fully to all that He promised.

Your acceptance of God and His commandments is all that is required for you to be in right relationship with God. There are no works that you must accomplish before He extends His promises of soul-satisfying, life-giving blessings.

Your relationship with God is not based upon your good deeds. It is not based upon your offering of a blood sacrifice at a designated shrine, your doing a series of charitable acts of kindness, or your belonging to a particular denomination. It is not based upon anything that you produce, achieve, or earn.

Rather, your relationship with God is based upon belief—your believing that Jesus Christ is God's Son come in the flesh and that Jesus Christ is Lord.

Behavior is the substance of religion. Belief is the substance of relationship.

You don't have to wonder if you have done enough to get good enough for God. You can say, "I believe in You, God, as the Giver of life. I believe in what Jesus did on the cross to give me life abundant and life forever. I accept Your plan!"

So many people I know live under a terrible cloud of "I hope I've done enough to please God." They hope they've read enough of the Bible and prayed enough. They hope God will forgive them. They hope they'll be considered worthy of heaven.

Such hope isn't true hope.

True hope lies in saying, "Thank You, God, for saving me! Thank You for loving me! Thank You for Jesus Christ and what He did for me on the cross! Thank You for giving me Your Holy Spirit to guide me and comfort me!"

Be very clear in your spirit on this point: your behavior and the state of your soul are two distinct things in God's eyes. Once you have accepted Jesus Christ as your Savior and have accepted God's love and forgiveness, you are His eternally. There is nothing that can separate you from Him. (See Rom. 8:38–39.)

The mistakes you make and the sins you commit after you have accepted Christ Jesus do not separate you from God. He will convict you of these sins so you can confess them, be forgiven, repent of them, and make a change in your future behavior—for your sake, for your good. But these sins do not separate you again from God. God told His people that even if they disobeyed Him and experienced all the negative consequences, He would still be there when they turned to Him. He continually called Himself "the LORD your God." They never ceased being His people.

Suppose you say, "Oh, God, I've really messed up. I know You're going to wipe me out today." Believe me when I tell you that God isn't going to pay any attention to what you say! Your behavior—including what you think and say—doesn't bring you into a state of condemnation.

Your relationship with God is based upon what Jesus has done, not what you have done, do now, or will do. It's solely based upon what Jesus did on the cross. You may make mistakes, but Jesus does not. You may be imperfect, but He is perfect. God's forgiveness is based upon His plan that has been fulfilled through Christ Jesus.

Ephesians 2:8 (NKJV) clearly states, "For by grace you have been saved through faith, and that not of yourselves; it is the gift of God." Receive His gift with your faith. Be assured that you have been saved and are in right relationship with Him.

God's plan for you is that you have assurance of your salvation and that you are loved by God.

Acceptance and Blessing

How does this relate to your receiving the fulfillment of God's promises of blessing in your life?

First, you must accept the fact that God desires to bless you.

You must stop accusing God and blaming God for the lack of substance or the troubles you experience. In many cases, you have brought upon yourself the consequences that you are experiencing. God makes it very clear in His Word that His desire is to bring about good things in your life, in the present and for all eternity.

Second, you must accept the fact that your sins are related to your blessings.

"But," you may be saying, "I thought you said that behavior had nothing to do with my relationship with God."

I did. Your good deeds can't earn you God's salvation, forgiveness, or love. Salvation is a free gift of God extended to you. You must only believe and receive in order to be saved and born again in your spirit.

As long as you continue in sin and refuse to accept God's offer of forgiveness, there's nothing God will do. He will not override your free will.

After you have accepted God's forgiveness, there is no amount of sin that can separate you from God's love. You have entered into a relationship with Him that is irreversible. At the same time, your behavior does influence the degree to which God can trust you with His blessings and to which He will reveal Himself to you. If you continue to ignore God, He will not force Himself upon you. If you continue to choose sinful behaviors over righteous behaviors, He will not ignore the consequences of sin and pour out to you a blessing.

Your behavior doesn't determine your relationship with God, but it does determine to a great extent the degree to which God can bless you.

Not too long ago I heard about a young woman who was very angry that a bank had not given her a loan that she desired. "I need that money to pay my bills," she said. "If I go into default on my house and car, it's the bank's fault."

She refused to accept the fact that she had terrible credit and was too great a risk for the bank. Her lack of funds wasn't the bank's fault. It was the fault of her overspending in the past.

When you face up to your sins and accept responsibility for your behavior and its related consequences, you then can turn to God and accept again His forgiveness for your sins. You can say to God, "Please help me not to do that again. Show me the way in which You want me to walk, and give me the courage and strength to walk in Your path." You can accept again the plan and purpose that God has for you.

If you fail to heed God's voice, you can turn to God, receive forgiveness, and begin again to listen to Him and to obey Him.

If you fail to keep His commandments, you can turn to God, receive forgiveness, and begin again to observe and keep His commandments.

If you have served false gods and given your time, talent, devotion, and respect to things or people above God, you can turn to God, receive forgiveness, and begin again to worship and serve God as your first priority.

The acceptance of God's way is your responsibility. When you accept Him, His acceptance of you is both certain and firm. You can always count on God to forgive you every time you ask Him for forgiveness.

A Lifestyle Marked by Availability

Through the Cross, God has made Himself totally available to you—sixty minutes an hour, twenty-four hours a day, every day of every year of your life.

Jesus invites you to come boldly into the throne room of God and to find grace and mercy for help in your times of need. He makes God completely accessible.

Anytime you have a need, problem, difficult question, doubt, or lack of substance in your life, you can turn to God immediately, make your request known, and receive His wisdom and His provision.

God's provision for you may come about in stages or steps. You may not receive immediately all that you request from Him, but the tide is turned the moment you turn to Him. Whenever you cast all of your care and concern upon Him and rely upon Him totally to supply your need and to show you how you are to live, He is quick to respond.

The woman I mentioned who had asked for and been denied a bank loan experienced this. A friend confronted her by saying, "It isn't the bank's fault you are in financial trouble. It's your own fault. If you want real help, you need to see a financial counselor."

The woman agreed to accept this form of help. She went with her friend to see a financial counselor, who had volunteered his services at her friend's church. The woman made a budget for the first time in her life. She faced her mountain of bills and mapped out a plan for paying them.

In the process, she allowed her car to be repossessed, and she used public transportation for six months while she could save for the purchase of a used car—one she later called a real "clunker." She gave up her home and moved into an apartment she could afford. Slowly but surely, she began to chip away at her debt. One of her favorite pastimes had been shopping. She decided that the best way to avoid overspending was to avoid shopping. She took on a part-time evening job as a diversion. She later said, "This took my eyes off all the commercials on TV, which really caused me to focus on material things, and it took me out of the mall." To her benefit, of course, was added income to pay against her debt. It took her two years of very diligent saving, paying bills, and working an extra fifteen hours a week to pay off all her bills.

Then she found that what she had been paying on her bills was money freed up to spend on a better car. After she had her car paid off, she began to save for a house. In all, it took her almost five years to completely turn around her financial situation to one where she had no indebtedness other than her mortgage and enough monthly income to pay her bills.

Was God at work in this? Most assuredly. The woman began to attend the church where she had received the free financial counseling, and she learned about God's plan for prospering her life. She began to tithe regularly and to get involved in outreach ministries at the church. She said about her activities in the church, "One day I realized that the things I enjoyed doing the most were things related to the church. And you know what? Most of those things were *free*. I had spent thousands of dollars a year on entertainment—on going places and doing things to try to have a good time and make friends. Now I was having a good time and making friends, and it wasn't costing me a dime!"

Was God available when this woman turned to Him for help? Absolutely.

Was His desire to bless her and bring her into greater prosperity and wholeness in every area of her life? Absolutely.

Did He begin to work immediately when she turned to Him for help? Absolutely.

Was her problem solved in a day? No. Was her problem solved in a way that brought glory to God and was of lasting and eternal benefit to her? Absolutely.

God is available to you whenever you turn to Him.

Stop to consider what Jesus did with His disciples and those who loved Him. He traveled with them. He watched them fish. He fixed breakfast for them by the side of the lake. He walked the dusty roads of the land with them. He had picnics with them on the hillsides of Galilee. He had supper with them. He washed their feet. He laughed with them and cried with them. Jesus made Himself totally accessible to His disciples while still maintaining His need for prayer and time alone with His heavenly Father. He even said about the little children who were brought to Him, "Don't stop them from coming to Me." Jesus had time for people.

Jesus didn't demand or require that His disciples bow to Him and give Him homage. He said to His disciples, "You aren't My servants. You are My friends!" (See John 15:15.)

Many people I've met assign these labels to God: *severe, condemning, stern, perfection-demanding taskmaster*. These words make God seem untouchable.

How about these words instead? *Tender, warm, loving*. That's the way we think of Jesus as He held little children and touched the sick and raised them to wholeness. Jesus said He was just like the Father. In fact, He said to His disciples, "If you've seen Me, you've seen the Father!" (See John 14:9.)

God is accessible to you today. So are the blessings He has for you. You may not receive them in an instant, but you can count on receiving them ultimately.

Make yourself accessible to God. Open up the areas of your life that you have tried to keep from Him. Let Him have all of you. As you make yourself accessible to God, He is able to pour more and more of Himself into you.

A Lifestyle Marked by Abundance

Jesus said that He came to give us an abundant life. (See John 10:10.) When we think of abundance today, many people use the word *prosperity*.

One of the foremost concepts you need to understand about prosperity is this: biblical prosperity relates to your entire life. A person can be rich in money and still not be prosperous. When you think of blessing and prosperity, you must think in terms of life's whole—a harmony that has spiritual, mental, emotional, physical, financial, and relational dimensions.

Many people have the mind-set that "my spiritual life is my spiritual life" and "my business life is my business life." They separate the two in their thinking and in their behavior. God, however, does not. From His perspective, the two are vitally and intricately connected. It is not possible to be fully prosperous in life if your spiritual life is lacking, just as it is not possible to be fully prosperous if you have a material or financial lack.

God is not opposed to your having money. Rather, He is opposed to anything that you make an idol or a false god in your life. He is opposed to your worship or love of money. Paul wrote to Timothy, "For the love of money is a root of all kinds of evil, for which some have strayed from the faith in their greediness, and pierced themselves through with many sorrows" (1 Tim. 6:10 NKJV).

Conversely, God is for your having your needs met. He receives no glory from His people suffering from lack of provision. Some people have misinterpreted the Word of God to believe that God condones poverty and has a special blessing for the poor. There is no blessing attached with poverty in the Scriptures. Jesus wants His followers to care for the poor, give to the poor, and recognize that the poor are with us, but His greater desire is that all men and women be blessed and made whole, including having financial needs met.

God has placed a number of rules regarding prosperity in His Word; among them are these:

- We are not to covet the wealth or possessions of others (Ex. 20:17).
- We are to stay away from greed (Prov. 1:16–19; 15:27).
- We are to shun laziness and work diligently (Prov. 20:4; Eccles. 9:10).
- We are to give generously to those in need (Luke 6:38; 1 Tim. 6:17–19).
- We are to avoid debt (Prov. 22:7; Rom. 13:8).
- We are to trust God fully for our provision and our prosperity (Prov. 11:28; 16:20).
- We are to recognize always that God is the Source of our total supply of provision (Ps. 34:8–10; James 1:17).

Prosperity is far from a matter of receiving only. It is related to your giving, your trust of God, and your attitude toward possessions.

The Blessing of Work

Part of God's blessing to us is work. Each of us has been given specific talents and abilities that God expects us to use in labor for His kingdom. Some of us are required to labor in full-time ministry. Some are called to be God's witnesses in the workplace, in the medical world, in the school systems, or in a wide variety of other careers. We are to use our talents fully and to trust God to multiply the fruit of our labor for His purposes.

Your place of employment, your employer, your supervisor, your clients, your patients, your students—all are blessings from God to you. They are His tools of provision for your life and also the ones to whom God desires to give *through you*. Again, they are part of God's plan for wholeness and total prosperity in your life—just as you are a part of His plan for wholeness and total prosperity in their lives.

One of the prayers I believe we are all wise to pray is that God will enlarge our usefulness—our capacity and ability to work. We do well to heed this proverb:

> *A man will be satisfied with good by the fruit of his mouth,*
> *And the recompense of a man's hands will be rendered to him.*
> (Prov. 12:14 NKJV)

God desires that we be rewarded fully for the work that we do.

The Lord also desires that we "increase more and more." Paul wrote to the Thessalonians,

> *We urge you, brethren, that you increase more and more; that you also aspire to lead a quiet life, to mind your own business, and to work with your own hands, as we commanded you, that you may walk properly toward those who are outside, and that you may lack nothing.* (1 Thess. 4:10–12 NKJV)

Part of increasing lies in your learning how to work smarter, faster, and more productively and efficiently. I firmly believe that God imparts His wisdom to you regarding your work whenever you ask Him.

Withholding from God

Many people miss out on the blessing of God's abundance because they withhold their substance from God. They refuse to give Him any of their material goods—their money, financial resources, or possessions. Some do this out of ignorance; others out of rebellion; others out of a lack of trust that God will meet their needs.

If you truly want to be blessed financially and to loosen the grip that money, or the lack of it, has over your life, you must be generous in your finances toward God. As in all other areas, the degree to which you open yourself to God in giving is the degree to which you open yourself to God for receiving. Jesus taught, "Freely you have received, freely give" (Matt. 10:8 NKJV). And in 2 Corinthians 9:6 (NKJV), we read, "He who sows sparingly will also reap sparingly, and he who sows bountifully will also reap bountifully."

Why does God ask us to give our money to His work? I believe that it is because, to a great extent, our money is a reflection of ourselves. Our giving is a reflection of the degree to which we trust God to supply what we need materially.

Malachi 3:8–12 (NKJV) is one of the clearest Bible passages about what God expects from us. It holds a conditional promise related to our financial and material well-being:

> *"Will a man rob God?*
> *Yet you have robbed Me!*
> *But you say,*
> *'In what way have we robbed You?'*
> *In tithes and offerings.*
> *You are cursed with a curse,*
> *For you have robbed Me,*
> *Even this whole nation.*
> *Bring all the tithes into the storehouse,*
> *That there may be food in My house,*
> *And try Me now in this,"*
> *Says the LORD of hosts,*
> *"If I will not open for you the windows of heaven*
> *And pour out for you such blessing*
> *That there will not be room enough to receive it.*

And I will rebuke the devourer for your sakes,
So that he will not destroy the fruit of your ground,
Nor shall the vine fail to bear fruit for you in the field,"
Says the LORD of hosts;
"And all nations will call you blessed,
For you will be a delightful land,"
Says the LORD of hosts.

The heartfelt desire of God is that He might be allowed to bless His people and rebuke the devourer. His very specific method toward this end is the tithe. The tithe, the first tenth of what you receive, is to be from your increase and for your increase. It is the way you open the door of your finances to give and then to receive God's blessing.

When you give the tithe to God, you must always remember, the tithe was never really yours in the first place! All things come from God, including this amount called the tithe. As 1 Chronicles 29:14 (NKJV) declares, "All things come from You. And of Your own we have given You." When you give the first tenth of your earnings back to God, you simply are returning to Him what was His in the first place, and you are asking Him to use your gift for your increase.

The tithe is a sign of your trust in God. It is a tangible sign that you are accepting what God has put forth as a commandment. You are obeying what God has said to do. The tithe, therefore, becomes something of a trigger that brings forth even more blessing. And what a blessing it is!

God will open the windows of heaven and pour out a blessing on you that is so great, you can't contain it all. Certainly, that blessing comes to you in the form of

- an abundance of innovative, creative ideas and insights.
- a fullness of joy and a positive attitude.
- an enhanced ability to communicate with others.
- an abundance of strength, energy, and physical vitality and health.

- new opportunities for work and investment.
- provision from unexpected sources.

Not only that, but God says He will rebuke the devourer. Your work will come to fruition. You will be spared many of the attacks of the enemy against your life and finances. In very practical ways this can mean the following:

- Less illness, and therefore fewer hours of lost productivity and less expense
- Fewer breakdowns in equipment, machinery, or vehicles
- Fewer obstacles or problems
- Fewer accidents or mishaps
- Fewer interruptions or delays

Along with this personal blessing, tithes bring a blessing to God's people. The work of the Lord is accomplished more speedily and effectively. Honor comes to God's people. The witness about God's goodness is expanded. The four blessings in this passage of Malachi may be summarized:

1. The promise of prosperity
2. The promise of plenty
3. The promise of protection
4. The promise of personal testimony

With God's blessing, of course, you always receive an increased awareness of God's presence. Your relationship with Him grows richer, deeper, more intimate, and more meaningful. God's blessings are bestowed upon you not only so that God might prove Himself faithful to you, but also so that He might draw you even nearer to Himself. That is the greatest form of abundance the human heart can fathom.

I have seen God's principle of abundance work in my life in numerous practical ways. This lesson about giving to God and receiving God's blessing was one of the first lessons I learned as a young man.

In my first job as a young teenager, I worked as a newspaper boy making $4 a week. I gave $1 a week to God's storehouse. I never would have dreamed of limiting myself to a mere forty cents. I was so grateful for the job and so pleased to be earning $4, it never crossed my mind to give back to God less than $1.

Shortly thereafter, I got a job—still as a newspaper boy—for $20 a week. That was a fivefold increase. Talk about the windows of heaven opening! Again, I gave back far more than 10 percent.

While I was working part-time in that job and going to high school, a man offered to help me attend college. I went to college with $75, and I left college not owing a cent. God richly and abundantly met my need. Once I had only a dime in my pocket, but I was never completely without money. And I never gave only 10 percent to God's work. I was in relationship with a God of abundance. My giving was born of gratitude, joy, and thanksgiving. My only regret was that I couldn't give more.

A Lifestyle Marked by Abiding in Him

Have you noticed a pattern in the receipt of God's blessings?

The more you accept what Jesus has done for you and what the Holy Spirit desires to do in you, the more you experience the loving and full acceptance of God.

The more you make yourself accessible to doing God's will, the more you experience the always accessible presence of God in your life.

The more you give to God with a cheerful heart and a willing hand, the more you experience God's abundance in every area of your life.

This opening of your entire life to God, and your receiving the fullness of God's life imparted to you, is a concept that Jesus called "abiding."

Jesus taught,

> *I am the true vine, and My Father is the vinedresser. Every branch in Me that does not bear fruit He takes away; and every branch that bears fruit He prunes, that it may bear more fruit. You are already clean because of the word which I have spoken to you. Abide in Me, and I in you. As the branch cannot bear fruit of itself, unless it abides in the vine, neither can you, unless you abide in Me. I am the vine, you are the branches. He who abides in Me, and I in him, bears much fruit; for without Me you can do nothing. If anyone does not abide in Me, he is cast out as a branch and is withered; and they gather them and throw them into the fire, and they are burned. If you abide in Me, and My words abide in you, you will ask what you desire, and it shall be done for you. By this My Father is glorified, that you bear much fruit; so you will be My disciples.*
> (John 15:1–8 NKJV)

I want you to notice several things about the abiding process.

First, you are to abide in Christ.

Your total identity is in Him. You don't presume to have any gifts, talents, or abilities apart from what God has given you. You don't presume to have any spiritual gifts apart from what the Holy Spirit imparts to you. You don't presume to have any goodness in yourself or any righteousness. Your life is totally and completely embedded within Christ and what He has accomplished and is accomplishing on your behalf. Jesus clearly says that apart from Him you can do nothing.

Abiding in Christ means that your total trust is in Him. You don't trust a college degree, a relationship with the boss, appearance, acquisition of material goods, family reputation, "connections," or any other thing to bring you success and fulfillment in Christ. Your total trust is in Christ and in His ability and desire to bring you to the place of success and fulfillment according to His definition and His plan.

Second, you are subject to pruning.

God's pruning process is described in the previous chapter, but notice here the reason for being pruned—that you might bear "much fruit." God's desire is for your good. He loves you enough to prune you. And He does so in order that you might increase and come to greater prosperity and wholeness.

This passage in John echoes what Jesus said earlier, "Unless a grain of wheat falls into the ground and dies, it remains alone; but if it dies, it produces much grain" (John 12:24 NKJV). Many seeds, much fruit. God's desire is to bless you more and more and more and more until you come to the place where you are into a spilling-over abundance of blessing that is beyond your ability to contain it.

Third, the fruit that you bear is His fruit, the result of your abiding.

God is doing a work of refinement and perfection in you. He is the One who decides which blessing you need at which time. He is the One who directs you to give to others so you might be a blessing to them.

Fourth, abiding is a matter of trust.

Much of the theology we hear today is self-centered and self-seeking: "God, I want You to heal me, prosper me, bless me, protect me. God, do this, this, this, and thus and so for me."

The truth is that we are not at the center of the universe. But God is, and He requires that we serve Him. We are highly presumptuous when we demand that He do our bidding as if He is our errand boy. The proper relationship with God is one in which we put ourselves into a position to do *His* bidding. He is the Lord God almighty!

When we look to God in any other way, we are into idolatry. When we do not seek the presence of God in us as much as we desire the things that we want God to do for us, we are not worshiping God nearly as much as we are worshiping the provision of God. We are worshiping the blessing instead of the Blessing Giver.

I cannot emphasize to you enough how subtle and insidious idolatry can be. I feel certain that if I asked you, "Do you want to be idolatrous?" you would answer with a resounding, "No!" Most of us, however, are wise to search our souls diligently. As we do, we very often discover that we have placed too much value on certain possessions or relationships, sometimes elevating them above our relationship with God.

A number of years ago, the church was facing a financial challenge, and I felt impressed that I should sell my camera equipment and give the money toward the pledge drive. Through the years, I had invested in top-quality cameras and various pieces of photographic equipment. Since I love to take photographs, I worked to become good at photography, and I took a certain amount of pride in the photographic equipment I purchased. My personal gift involved the one possession that I cherished the most.

To my surprise, I felt a certain amount of pain in making my gift. As much as I wanted to make the gift in my mind, the actual giving of the gift—the day I took the cameras down to the camera store and turned them in for cash—was a tough experience. I hadn't been aware that it was going to be one of God's pruning experiences in my life.

I had to face the fact that I valued the cameras too much. Once I gave the cameras—not only in a literal sense but in my spirit—I felt a great release. He was going to use my gift to help resolve the need in the church, and He was going to use my gift to resolve a need in *me*. He was going to strip away from me my grip on this tangible, material substance that I held to be important.

As it turned out, once I had truly given my cameras to God in my heart and had surrendered myself anew in this area of my life, He dealt in a sovereign way to restore my cameras and equipment to me. They then became to me a gift from God—they were no longer solely something that I had purchased and owned as the result of my own planning and effort. God had turned them into a gift from *Him*.

I have seen this same principle work in the lives of countless people. When God prunes away something in our lives, He causes us to experience or to receive something far more valuable or beneficial. Even more important, spiritual fruit is produced in us. We gain more of the nature of Christ, more of the power of the Holy Spirit, more of the qualities of character that are eternal. Nothing is more valuable to us than our obedience to God and our trust in Him. When we yield ourselves fully to Him, He pours Himself fully into us.

God will not allow you to abide in anything other than Himself, or allow anything other than His Holy Spirit to abide in you, because God will not allow you to place your trust in anything but Him. He will prune away at you until you come to total submission to His will and total reliance upon His presence and power flowing in you.

Fifth, abiding is subject to conditional consequences.

Jesus taught that if you don't abide, you will be separated from His flow of blessings. If you do abide, you can ask for what you desire and receive it. The fact is, if you truly are abiding in God's Word—listening to God, reading and obeying His commandments, giving up idols—then your desires are going to be God's desires for you. They won't be self-centered, selfish desires. They will be desires that are totally in keeping with God's plan for you. Your desires will reflect the very character of the Holy Spirit in you.

Pruning brings you to the place of desiring only things that are of God.

Once again, the more you abide in Christ, the more He abides in you.

A Lifestyle Marked by Accountability

Alife of blessing is marked by accountability for your actions. God desires that you be His witness in your sphere of influence. You are responsible for knowing God, experiencing Him, and reflecting Him.

How can you know God? You know Him primarily by reading His Word and communicating with Him in prayer—not only talking to God but listening to Him.

How can you experience God? You can wait on the Holy Spirit to assure you that the words you speak, the decisions you make, and the actions you undertake are right in His sight. He will make Himself known to you if you put yourself in a position before Him to listen to Him and wait for His guidance.

The more you seek to know God and to rely upon God, the more He reveals Himself to you. And the more He reveals Himself to you, the more you automatically reflect Him to others. You don't have to work up a spiritual résumé or strive to perform good works on God's behalf. You can trust God to bring to you the people to whom He wants you to speak and on whose behalf He wants you to take specific actions or to lead you to them.

Your witness is your life. It is reflected in everything you say and do. It is a normal part of your life. Your conversations are naturally sprinkled with the name of Jesus. In fact, you don't even have to think about bringing up His name. Your relationship with Him is something that you are totally at ease in sharing with others. His life becomes your life.

One of the things that the Holy Spirit does in you is to convict you about habits that you need to change so that you might reflect greater glory to God. The Holy Spirit points out to you the things you have done about which you need to apologize or seek to make amends with others. The Holy Spirit calls you continually to accountability—to a full recognition of and responsibility for what you say and do.

Each of us is called to self-judgment. God asks us to evaluate ourselves against the standard of His Word and the life of Jesus Christ. We are called to aim the searchlight onto our souls.

Every time we come to an area of our lives about which we must confess, "This is not what Jesus would do," we are to ask God to help us repent of our old ways and to adopt the behavior that He desires for us to manifest.

This is a lifelong process. No one ever arrives at full perfection. We will always find something more within us that needs to be cleansed and refined.

In recent years, I have been through intense personal struggle. I have had to confront a number of things in my life—things that I had tended to ignore over the years and things that turned out to be very painful for me to face. We all like to think we're on the road to being perfect, and I believe it's always painful when we realize just how imperfect we are.

Some of what I had to face were experiences and painful memories associated with my childhood. I had excess baggage that I needed to release to God in order to experience a genuine healing and a greater understanding of God's love.

In addition, I have had to face my frustration that life has not gone the way I desired it to go. I have had to deal with circumstances and situations that have been beyond my ability to control or to determine their outcome. Each time one of these situations has arisen, I have found myself in a position of having to choose—either to let God do things His way or to struggle to make things happen my way. I know that letting God do things His way is the course to take, but that doesn't make it any easier. There has been a pruning away of many dead branches in my life.

All of this is a process of accountability. God expects me to face the reality of my life so that I might truly face the reality of His life— a life of unlimited power, wisdom, love, and presence. He is everlasting and unchanging.

Our accountability is for ourselves before God and also an accountability to others in the body of Christ. God calls upon us to be vulnerable to others, to be in a giving and receiving relationship with them: "Confess your trespasses to one another, and pray for one another, that you may be healed" (James 5:16 NKJV).

God loves you too much to allow you to live in an isolation chamber, a state that can quickly lead to your living at one of two extremes. Either you will have a tendency to feel great loneliness and to suffer from feelings of rejection, or you will have a tendency to become self-righteous and highly critical of others. Instead, God desires that you know the blessing of human love—that you be willing to extend love to others and to receive love from others. As you confess your faults and weaknesses to others, and pray for and with others, you are healed.

Your accountability to others requires you

- to be honest with yourself and then with others.
- to value yourself and to value others.
- to tell the truth to yourself so that you might tell the truth in love to others.
- to pursue the excellence of Christ's nature so that you might help others to experience His presence more fully in their lives.

Accountability insists that you face your faults, and face them *first* before confronting the faults of others. Jesus taught, "Why do you look at the speck in your brother's eye, but do not consider the plank in your own eye?" (Matt. 7:3 NKJV).

Accountability requires that you forgive others so that you might receive forgiveness from God and be able to forgive yourself. (See Luke 6:37.)

What does accountability have to do with experiencing God's blessings? Everything! Unless you are willing to face up to the things in your life that keep you from accepting God's forgiveness, keep you from obeying God's commandments, keep you from making yourself accessible to God, hinder you from abiding in Christ, and cause you to remain outside the flow of God's abundance, you will not take the steps you need to take in order to experience the fullness of God's outpoured blessing.

Unless you are willing to face your sin, you won't repent of it and know an increase of God's power and presence flowing in you.

Unless you are willing to yield to God's pruning, you won't bear much fruit.

And until you are willing to face up to your faults and to submit them to prayer, you cannot be healed and made whole.

The good news is that the more you seek to be accountable for your life, the more the Lord blesses your relationship with Him and your relationships with others.

Hope for a Blessed Future

What does all of this have to do with hope?

If you are in a state of expectation that God still has good things to pour into your life and through your life to others, you are going to have a hope that you can hardly contain! You are going to envision a bright future that's worthy of your anticipation.

When you know with certainty in your spirit that God is totally accepting of you because you are forgiven and in right relationship with Him, you live without the heaviness of guilt or self-condemnation. You have the freedom to explore all of God's creation and all of the opportunities that He sends your way.

When you make yourself accessible to God and know with certainty that He is always accessible to you, you have greater freedom and boldness to talk to God about what He desires for you.

When you know that God has abundance for you, you are more eager to live in such a way that you qualify fully for all of God's blessings.

When you are abiding in Christ, you have a wonderful sense of security.

When you hold yourself accountable, you are open to the changes that God desires to make in your life for your good.

In all these ways, you put yourself into a position to receive more of God's presence and power at work in your life. You can say with confidence,

---

I have hope because all of God's promises are intended for me, and He still has blessings to give to me.

CHAPTER 9

GOD'S EVER-PRESENT HELP

Julie, a single mother in her late twenties, recently met with one of my associates and said, "I need your help. I can't feel God anymore."

He asked, "Have you ever felt God in your life?"

"Oh, yes," she said. "I accepted Jesus as my Savior when I was a teenager at a retreat sponsored by my church youth group. I went to a Christian college, and I felt God in a powerful way in my life all through college. We had some wonderful chapel services, and I was part of a prayer group in my dormitory that was very meaningful to me. My college years were ones of real spiritual growth. I went to lots of retreats and seminars where the presence of God was really awesome. When I got married, I felt God in my life. I really felt He had brought my husband and me together. And I felt Him at work in my life when my two daughters were born. But I don't feel Him now."

"How did it feel to have God in your life?" my associate asked.

Julie reflected for a moment and then said, "I had a lot of peace in my life. I really wasn't worried about the future. Somehow I knew God was going to take care of things. I also had a lot of purpose. I felt that every day with God was a brand-new adventure. I could hardly wait to see what He would bring into my life. I just knew He was going to send interesting people and ideas and challenges my way. I was always looking for God's next word to me or for a way to share the gospel with other people. Life was exciting, even when on the surface my life may have looked as if it was fairly boring and predictable."

My associate asked, "And how do you feel now?"

"Dead inside," she said. Her tone of voice matched her words. "Nothing much interests me. Nothing excites me. Every day seems like the same old grind—get up, get my daughters ready to go to day care, go to work, pick up the girls, come home, fix dinner, wash the dishes, do a load of laundry, put out our clothes and prepare our lunches for the next day, and collapse into bed. I try to spend a few minutes praying and reading my Bible before I go to sleep, but I've got to confess, on lots of nights I fall asleep with my glasses on and the Bible next to me in the bed. On weekends, I run myself ragged on Saturdays cleaning house and doing all of the shopping errands that need to be done. On Sundays we go to church and Sunday school, and I spend the afternoon catching up on things I need to do so I'm ready for Monday morning. It's the same routine, week in and week out."

My associate then asked, "When did you stop feeling God at work in your life?"

Julie paused for a minute and then said sadly, "The day my husband walked out on us."

Julie had not at all made her husband out to be God in her life. She had a very clear understanding in her heart and mind that her husband was *not* the source of her life, nor was he her ultimate provider of happiness or material goods.

What her husband had been for her was a companion and a coworker in the care of their home and children. When he walked out and began living with another woman, Julie was left with sole responsibility for every aspect of the life they had started building together. All of the chores related to their married life became her chores. If the lawn was going to get mowed, she had to mow it. If the banking was to be done, she had to do it. If the laundry was to get done, she had to do it. If the bills needed to be paid, she had to pay them. If the car broke down, she had to figure out transportation and car repairs.

With sole responsibility came a great emotional and spiritual burden. Julie admitted as her conversation with my associate continued, "It's all on my shoulders. If my girls have lack of any kind in their lives, it's my fault. I have to be both mother and father to them. I have to take care of myself. I don't know how other women do it, and I don't have time to talk to them to find out!"

Julie had been divorced for two years, so she pretty much had moved beyond her initial anger and hurt at her husband's betrayal. What she felt was exhaustion—physical, mental, emotional, and spiritual. She had taken on a load that was too big for her to carry, a load that God never intended for her to carry alone.

In several key ways, she didn't feel God in her life because without thinking about it, and without intending to do so, she had taken over God's job. She felt totally responsible for making her life happen—for providing for herself and her children, for making certain that her children were safe and healthy, for doing her best to make her children happy and loved.

Not only did she no longer feel God in her life, but she resented God's absence. She said, "I feel as if He walked out and didn't leave a forwarding address. He left me to sort out my problems by myself."

If you are feeling today what Julie was feeling—abandoned, alone, overburdened—I have good news for you: God *is* present and available! The challenge you face is in seeing Him at work in ways that you previously haven't experienced.

The Answer to the "Why Me?" Question

So often in times of affliction, heartache, and suffering, we ask, "Why me?" Another way of asking that question is, "Where's

God?" Our line of reasoning is that if God truly cares about us and loves us as His children, He will protect us from all pain or need. When we find ourselves in one of life's trials, we automatically assume that God is absent.

God's Word says otherwise.

David wrote,

> *Yea, though I walk through the valley of the shadow of death,*
> *I will fear no evil;*
> *For You are with me;*
> *Your rod and Your staff, they comfort me.*
> *You prepare a table before me in the presence of my enemies.*
>
> (Ps. 23:4–5 NKJV)

David had full assurance that in the most dangerous and fearful of situations, God was with him. In the presence of enemies who were out to destroy his life, God was there to provide for him.

God was with Daniel, even in a lions' den.

God was with Joseph in a desert pit, in a foreign land, in a prison dungeon.

God was with Moses, even when he was in exile and living on the back side of the desert.

God was with Ruth, even as she tried to make her way as a young widow in a strange land.

God was with the children of Israel, even as they crossed the Red Sea with Pharaoh's armies approaching rapidly from behind them.

God was with Esther, even as she risked her life to confront the man who was intent upon destroying her and her people.

God was with Jesus, even as He hung on the cross and lay in the tomb.

God is *always* with you.

At no time do we find in Scripture that God promises to change circumstances just because we want Him to do so. Rather, He promises to be with us in every circumstance and never to leave us or forsake us.

The Lesson of God's Sufficiency

The apostle Paul knew this well, and he wrote about it:

And lest I should be exalted above measure by the abundance of the revelations, a thorn in the flesh was given to me, a messenger of Satan to buffet me, lest I be exalted above measure. Concerning this thing I pleaded with the Lord three times that it might depart from me. And He said to me, "My grace is sufficient for you, for My strength is made perfect in weakness." Therefore most gladly I will rather boast in my infirmities, that the power of Christ may rest upon me. Therefore I take pleasure in infirmities, in reproaches, in needs, in persecutions, in distresses, for Christ's sake. For when I am weak, then I am strong. (2 Cor. 12:7–10 NKJV)

Paul knew what it was to suffer for the gospel, but perhaps the greatest pain he experienced was his suffering related to a "thorn in the flesh." God had delivered Paul from all other dangers, trials, and turmoils—God had brought him through shipwreck, muggings, hunger and thirst, beatings, imprisonment, a stoning, and other dramatic and traumatic experiences. God had *not* delivered him, however, from this trouble.

Paul never defined the thorn. We can conclude from the words that he chose to describe his affliction that it was something that struck his human nature—either his body or his emotions—not something that struck his spiritual relationship with God. And we can assume that it was an affliction that caused him great pain.

The type of thorn related to this word in the original Greek language is not a little sticker or briar that a person might pick up while walking barefoot. It is a thorn that is more like a long, sharp needle, extremely painful in its penetration. The thorn causes a sharp, jabbing pain that leaves a long-lasting ache even after the thorn is removed.

Paul agonized. He suffered. The thorn in the flesh was not a temporary or surface-level pain. Paul was deeply wounded.

Paul said several things about the thorn that are important for you today.

God allowed Paul to experience a thorn in the flesh.

Paul was writing to the Corinthians about his authority as an apostle. He spoke of having had profound visions and revelations of the Lord that he knew were from God, including one experience in which he felt caught up to heaven and had a vision of paradise that was far more glorious than anything on earth and that he could not fully describe in human language.

Paul wrote that he refrained from talking too much about his visions and revelations because he didn't want people to see him as anything other than a human being and a fellow servant of Christ Jesus. He didn't want personal adoration. He saw his thorn in the flesh as one way that God kept him from being worshiped for having experienced such a divine revelation of paradise. He wrote, "Lest I should be exalted above measure by the abundance of the revelations, a thorn in the flesh was given to me" (2 Cor. 12:7 NKJV).

Paul called this thorn a "messenger of Satan." Even so, God allowed Satan to give Paul this message, this affliction, again "lest I should be exalted above measure" (2 Cor. 12:7 NKJV).

God did not cause Julie, the young woman who met with my associate, to be divorced. Divorce was not a part of God's plan for her life. Her divorce was the result of an act of sin and rebellion on the part of her husband, followed by his willful decision to destroy their marriage. At the same time, God allowed the experience to happen in her life and in her husband's life. He could have struck her husband dead or perhaps have intervened with a serious form of punishment or affliction in his life, but God chose to allow the man to divorce his wife.

From my perspective, God's allowing that was nothing more than God's allowing a human being to make a bad decision. God does not override the human will. He allows us to make choices, even harmful and wrong ones. Much of what we blame God for doing is actually the result of our doing, our exertion of free will.

I recently heard a story about a man who asked God, with great concern and agony of spirit, why God allowed little children to be abused. The only thing he heard God say back to his spirit was this: *Why, oh, why, do men and women abuse little children?* The fault for the abuse of little children does not lie with God; it lies in the utter blackness of evil hearts.

I know a young woman who was diagnosed several months ago with bone cancer; she experienced breast cancer several years ago, and her physicians believed the bone cancer was a recurrence of that disease. She said, "One of my first questions was, 'Why me?' As I thought about my experiences with cancer, I realized that my cancer was probably related to several factors in my life—none of which were my fault. I had been exposed to a high degree of radiation at one point in my life. I spent several years living in another area that was later declared an environmental cleanup site because of toxic wastes. Furthermore, I have a history of breast cancer in my family. The more appropriate question to ask would have been, 'Why *not* me?'

"One out of four people will experience cancer in his or her life, according to today's statistics," she said. "The question of *why* is an important one for scientists, but I'm not a scientist—just a patient, a victim. The only question that really matters in my life is this one: 'What now?' And the only good answer that I have for that question—the only one that gives me any peace at all—is this: 'God is with me.'"

Whatever God has allowed to happen in your life, He is present with you in the midst.

God did not answer Paul's prayer as Paul wanted it answered.

Paul said, "Concerning this thing I pleaded with the Lord three times that it might depart from me" (2 Cor. 12:8 NKJV). Paul was praying for a complete and lasting healing. God didn't answer his prayer the way Paul wanted it answered.

Does that mean that you shouldn't bother to pray when you are struck with an affliction or hit with a crisis? Not at all. God expects you to pray, to make your requests known to Him. Jesus taught that you "always ought to pray and not lose heart" (Luke 18:1 NKJV). Paul told the Thessalonians to "pray without ceasing" (1 Thess. 5:17 NKJV).

Furthermore, you should call upon others who have faith to pray for you. "Is anyone among you suffering? Let him pray. Is anyone cheerful? Let him sing psalms. Is anyone among you sick? Let him call for the elders of the church, and let them pray over him, anointing him with oil in the name of the Lord" (James 5:13–14 NKJV).

Paul often wrote, "Brethren, pray for us" (1 Thess. 5:25; 2 Thess. 3:1 NKJV). The writer to the Hebrews noted the desired results of prayer: "Pray for us. . . . I especially urge you to do this, that I may be restored to you the sooner" (Heb. 13:18–19 NKJV).

Yes, you are to pray when afflictions strike you. But as you pray, you always must be willing for God to answer your prayers in His way, for His purposes, and in His timing.

God's answers include "no" answers to what you want. When you get a "no" answer or perhaps a "wait" answer—which is also something you probably in your impatience don't desire—you must be willing to accept that answer with the full confidence that God is sovereign, God is omniscient, and God is always precise.

In other words,

- *God knows what is best for you and for others*. He will do what is for your eternal best, not just what is for your temporary good.
- *God can enact His will*. He has all power and authority over His creation, and He can suspend even His own laws of creation if such a suspension suits His purposes.
- *God is never too early or too late*. He knows when and how He desires to make His will known.

You can never see things as fully as God sees them. You are a finite creature with a very limited understanding of God's methods. Isaiah declared God's truth,

> *For as the heavens are higher than the earth,*
> *So are My ways higher than your ways,*
> *And My thoughts than your thoughts.* (Isa. 55:9 NKJV)

God's perspective is the only one that counts. God's methods are the only ones that will work, ultimately and eternally. And God is absolutely and utterly faithful and trustworthy. You can trust Him to do what is best for you.

Of course, you should take action for your own good. God has entrusted many people with wisdom and skills to help you in times of trouble or need. You should avail yourself of all the help you can get—trusting at all times that God is working through these helpers on your behalf. If you get "bad help," you can ask God to point you toward "good help." You are to do everything that you know to do, and then trust God to do what only He can do.

Paul was brought to that point. God did not answer him in the way Paul desired to be answered. *But God did answer.*

God's answer for Paul was grace.

As I expressed in an earlier chapter, grace is God's work in you that you have done nothing to deserve or earn. It is His sovereign work. It includes His abiding presence.

Grace is God's answer to your pain and affliction whether He chooses, or doesn't choose, to change your circumstances. Regardless of the external forces that strike you or the consequences of evil assault that may be manifested against your life, God's presence abides with you. Paul wrote that the Lord spoke to him, "My grace is sufficient for you, for My strength is made perfect in weakness" (2 Cor. 12:9 NKJV).

In other words, God assured Paul, "I'm with you in this. In the areas where you are weak, I will show My strength." The result was that as Paul allowed God to become his strength, Paul became an even greater witness to those who knew him. Paul was able to conclude, "When I am weak, then I am strong" (2 Cor. 12:10 NKJV).

A woman whose mother died a slow and painful death with a debilitating muscle disease once said to me, "Dr. Stanley, I prayed and prayed for God to heal my mother. When she died, I felt at first that God had failed to answer my prayer. Then it occurred to me that God *had* healed my mother. He had removed her from anything Satan could do to her. She was safe and whole and fully healed in His presence forever! She would never know another hour of pain. If He had healed her, who knows what future disease she might have had that might have been even more painful or dreadful to her? My mother's great hope for her old age was that she would never lose her ability to think. She died with a sound mind, a keen sense of humor, and all of her mental faculties. She died surrounded by family and friends who loved her dearly. There was a great deal I found to be thankful for in her death."

I rejoiced with her at God's mercy, but there was more. She continued, "That isn't all that I discovered about God's methods. About six months after Mom's death, I began to receive reports from first this family member and then that one. They told me how much my mother had inspired them and how each time they had come to visit her or comfort her, they had left encouraged or helped.

"Friends of my mother called to share with me how much Mom had meant to them and how great her witness had been. One of her friends said, 'Your mother had faith to endure great pain and suffering, and I knew as I watched her go through her struggle so bravely, and always with the name of Jesus on her lips, that I didn't have that source of strength in my life. I gave my life to Christ because of the way your mother lived, but even more so, because of the way your mother died.'

"Another person, a cousin of mine, said, 'I had never thought about death until your mother was diagnosed with this disease. The way she approached death—as a homegoing, more than a departure—made me think about how I would face death. I came to grips with the fact that I wasn't ready to die. I gave my heart to the Lord.'

"In all, Dr. Stanley, I know of at least half a dozen people who gave their hearts to Christ because of my mother's witness while she was in the process of dying. My mother's great prayer was always that she would be a faithful witness for Christ. She was!"

The woman was glowing as she told me how thrilled she was that friends and relatives had come to the Lord through her mother's death. She concluded, "Dr. Stanley, God had a purpose for my mother's illness. Not only is Mom safely with the Lord now, but at least six other people are also going to be safely with the Lord after they die. Who knows how many they may influence for Christ before they go to be with Mom and Jesus?"

God's grace was sufficient for that dear woman. And it is sufficient for you.

God's Covenant with His People

God's covenant with each one of us is that He is always available to us, and He is always accepting of us.

There are no circumstances that can draw God away from us.

I heard a person say, "God's too busy for me to bother Him with my problem."

Nothing could be farther from the truth. God always has time for His children. He always responds to us with love.

A favorite chapter in the Bible for many people is 1 Corinthians 13, which we discussed in chapter 4. It is often called the Love Chapter and is frequently read at weddings. In that chapter, Paul described the nature of love and, more specifically, the nature of *God's* love. The love he depicted is often ascribed to or interpreted as human love, which I did in an earlier chapter. At an even deeper spiritual level, it is also a description of God's great love for us. We human beings can't love as Paul described without God's love pouring into and through our hearts. God empowers the kind of love Paul wrote about:

> *Love suffers long and is kind; love does not envy; love does not parade itself, is not puffed up; does not behave rudely, does not seek its own, is not provoked, thinks no evil; does not rejoice in iniquity, but rejoices in the truth; bears all things, believes all things, hopes all things, endures all things. Love never fails.* (1 Cor. 13:4–8 NKJV)

Most of us would love to claim that we have someone in our lives who loves us like this—someone who is always patient with us, isn't envious of us, thinks of us first, believes in us, hopes for us, endures hard times with us. What a wonderful thing to be loved like that!

The truth is, God loves us like that.

God doesn't keep a scoreboard when it comes to love. He doesn't respond in love to you only if you first respond in love to Him. No, God is always the initiator of love in your life. He makes Himself available to you not because of your need but because He has chosen to make Himself available. He is accepting of you not because of anything you have done or not done, but because He has chosen to love you.

You never walk life's road alone if you have Christ in your life. It is impossible to do so. He is with you even if you don't acknowledge His presence.

Three Manifestations
of God's Presence

God manifests His abiding ever-present help to you in three significant ways.

1. He delivers you from evil.

Jesus taught His disciples to pray, "Deliver us from the evil one" (Matt. 6:13 NKJV). God may not deliver you directly from every circumstance that you consider to be bad—just as He did not deliver Paul completely from his thorn in the flesh—but God always delivers you from Satan, the devil, the evil one.

The three friends of Daniel—Shadrach, Meshach, and Abed-Nego—knew this to be true. When King Nebuchadnezzar built an image of gold to himself and set it up on the plain just outside Babylon, he ordered that at the sound of a specific song, all people were to bow down and worship the image. Shadrach, Meshach, and Abed-Nego, who had been taught from birth never to worship anyone but the Lord God, refused to obey the new law.

Nebuchadnezzar threatened to have them thrown into a fiery furnace and then offered them a second chance to bow. They answered King Nebuchadnezzar in this way:

> *O Nebuchadnezzar, we have no need to answer you in this matter. If that is the case, our God whom we serve is able to deliver us from the burning fiery furnace, and He will deliver us from your hand, O king. But if not, let it be known to you, O king, that we do not serve your gods, nor will we worship the gold image which you have set up.* (Dan. 3:16–18 NKJV)

What a great proclamation of faith by the three men who seemed to be facing a sure death sentence! Note carefully what they said.

First, they said, "We don't even have to think about our answer in this matter." They were 100 percent committed to worshiping only God and to keeping His commandments. There was never any doubt, no choice to be weighed.

The more you allow the Lord to be present with you and to give you His daily guidance, the more you will know with clarity and certainty the way in which God wants you to walk. You won't have any doubt about whether something is sinful or not. You will know when you are tempted to engage in activities or behavior that God considers to be evil.

A teenager asked her mother how she might say no to her friends when they tried to talk her into doing things that she knew were wrong. Her mother said, "Look them right in the eye and ask, 'Are you nuts?' Then walk away. Don't debate the issue."

That's good advice when it comes to the temptations of Satan. In most cases, you don't need to struggle with him or engage in a debate. Rather, you need to resist him and walk away toward the good things God puts before you. Shadrach, Meshach, and Abed-Nego couldn't walk away, but they did refuse to argue the situation or reconsider their stance. Their minds were made up regarding their relationship with God.

Second, Shadrach, Meshach, and Abed-Nego said, "Our God is able to deliver us from the furnace." They had no doubt that God could deliver them if He wanted to do so. Bear in mind that furnace was extremely hot. It was intended to reduce to ashes those who disobeyed the king's order. The blaze was no doubt roaring in their ears even as they made the claim about God's power.

There are times when the roar of evil is so great all around you that you can feel the heat of hell lapping at your heels. There seems to be no escape. That is the time to say, "Our God is able!" Nothing is beyond His power. No disease, no situation, no circumstance, no tragedy is beyond His ability to heal, restore, or resolve.

Third, Shadrach, Meshach, and Abed-Nego declared, "And He will deliver us from your hand, O king." The three Hebrew men had absolutely no question that God would deliver them from evil, which at that moment was embodied by the king. They said, "God is able to deliver us from the furnace, but God *will* deliver us from you."

That is the stance we must take toward Satan and the evil he sends our way. I feel certain it is the stance that Paul took when it came to his thorn in the flesh. God *can* deliver us from the evil circumstances we are experiencing, but without a doubt, He *will* deliver us from Satan, the author of evil.

A bad situation may remain in your life. You may have to go through the furnace, just as Shadrach, Meshach, and Abed-Nego eventually did. Things may get worse before they get better. But God's promise to deliver you from evil assures you that the bad situation *will have no eternal consequence in your life.*

A couple of years ago I read a news report about a young man who had been imprisoned for the brutal murder of his parents. He had been involved in a satanic cult and had been under the influence of drugs at the time he committed the crime. After he was imprisoned and was facing a death sentence, a Christian couple shared the gospel with him. He gave his life to Christ and was marvelously saved.

The young man hadn't accepted Christ in hopes that his conversion might alter his future. He was still imprisoned on death row. He didn't try to win sympathy or justify his right to live. Rather, he said, "I am in prison for what I have done, and rightfully so. I committed a terrible crime and the consequence for it is death. The hope that I have is that my life doesn't end with a lethal injection. From that moment on, my life is with God in heaven. Nothing about my circumstance has changed or will change because of my commitment to Christ, but everything about my future has changed."

The young man had faced the fact that God was not going to deliver him from his circumstances, but that God had and would deliver him from evil.

Fourth, Shadrach, Meshach, and Abed-Nego concluded, "Even if God doesn't deliver us from the furnace, O king, we won't disobey Him. We will not serve any god other than the Lord God almighty."

Paul echoed that stance of faith: "If Christ appears stronger in my life because of this thorn, then so be it. I will be glad for this infirmity. In fact, if any infirmity, reproach, need, persecution, or distress in my life can bring greater glory to Christ, then bring it on. I will gladly experience it and even take pride in it." (See 2 Cor. 12:9–10.)

God will deliver you from evil as you trust Him with your life. You may have to go through deep waters, but the good news is that you will go through them. He has a victory for you on the other side, a victory untainted by evil.

You may be knocked down, but you won't be destroyed eternally.

You may have hard times, but your spirit will triumph.

You may know pain and suffering, but God will deliver you from the evil one.

The outcome is certain. God will win, and because He wins and you are in Him, you will win too. You may arrive bruised and battered at heaven's gate, but you *will arrive* at heaven's gate.

2. He helps you to endure and to overcome.

As you go through difficult times and assaults from the enemy of your soul, God strengthens you to endure and to overcome.

In describing future persecutions, Jesus said to His disciples, "You will be hated by all for My name's sake. But he who endures to the end will be saved" (Matt. 10:22 NKJV).

When trouble strikes, that's the time to burrow into God. So many people reject God and run from God when hard times come their way. They need to reverse their direction and run toward God! He is the Source of their strength, their ability to endure.

The more difficult your experience and the greater the challenges, the more time you need to spend with God.

"But where will I find the time?" you may ask.

If you don't spend sufficient time with the Lord, you will be overwhelmed by life, and all of the time that you do have will be filled with stress, frustration, and a series of failures.

Some of the busiest and most productive people for the gospel through the centuries have been men and women who spent hours every day in prayer and reading the Scriptures. The greater the call of God on their lives to give of themselves, the greater their need to receive from Him first.

To endure and overcome means to outlast. It means that when the trouble comes to an end—and certainly, no trouble lasts forever—you are still standing in faith, declaring that Jesus is Lord over all.

Part of what you are called to overcome in your life is not things that come at you from the outside—the external assaults that batter against your life. Much of what you must overcome lies within.

The Lord gave John a specific word to the seven churches that were under his leadership. To each of the churches, the Lord had a word of encouragement and also a word of warning. The concluding word to each church was along these lines:

- He who has an ear, let him hear what the Spirit says.
- He who overcomes shall be rewarded.

The situation in each church was different. So was the reward for overcoming. The theme, however, was constant. The churches were to confront not only the evil assault that was aimed at them from without, but also the insidious evil that had crept within. The Lord called them to be faithful in their relationship with Christ and to repent of their wrongdoing and sinful attitudes.

The Lord calls you to the same position. He will strengthen you to endure the assaults from Satan and He will help you to overcome the error of your ways, but you must be willing to stand against Satan and to repent of your sins.

Your part is to make a choice for God. His part is to reward your faithfulness in such a way that your choice is solidified and stands fast all the way to eternity.

3. He imparts mercy for each new circumstance you face.

The prophet Jeremiah was no stranger to adversity. He lived at a time when the children of Israel were being taken into bondage. Jeremiah knew that there would be no reversal of the situation and that hard times were coming—and in his later writings, were already at hand. Even so, Jeremiah wrote,

> This I recall to my mind,
> Therefore I have hope.
> Through the LORD's mercies we are not consumed,
> Because His compassions fail not.
> They are new every morning;
> Great is Your faithfulness.
> "The LORD is my portion," says my soul,
> "Therefore I hope in Him!"
> The LORD is good to those who wait for Him,
> To the soul who seeks Him.
> It is good that one should hope and wait quietly
> For the salvation of the LORD. (Lam. 3:21–26 NKJV)

Every day has new challenges. Jesus taught that you are to trust God daily to meet your needs, and then He said, "Sufficient for the day is its own trouble" (Matt. 6:34 NKJV). As a Christian, you are not spared life's troubles. You experience the same trials and difficulties and problems as those who don't know Christ. The difference is that you have God's mercy.

Even as troubles come to you on a daily basis, so do God's mercies. As Jeremiah proclaimed, "His mercies are new every morning." No matter what comes your way, God has already arranged a sufficient amount of mercy to cover that problem. God's mercy is a continually renewable resource.

Therefore, you can join with Jeremiah in declaring about God, "Great is Your faithfulness!"

Most Christians have sung the hymn that is based upon this passage from Lamentations. The lyrics can inspire hope in even the gloomiest and direst situations:

Great is Thy faithfulness, O God my Father,
There is no shadow of turning with Thee;
Thou changest not, Thy compassions, they fail not;
As Thou hast been, Thou forever wilt be.

Summer and winter and springtime and harvest,
Sun, moon, and stars in their courses above,
Join with all nature in manifold witness
To Thy great faithfulness, mercy and love.

Pardon for sin and a peace that endureth,
Thine own dear presence to cheer and to guide;
Strength for today and bright hope for tomorrow,
Blessings all mine, with ten thousand beside!

Great is Thy faithfulness!
Great is Thy faithfulness!
Morning by morning new mercies I see;
All I have needed Thy hand hath provided—
Great is Thy faithfulness, Lord, unto me.

—Thomas Chisholm
"Great Is Thy Faithfulness"

Are you facing a difficult time now? Turn to the One who is with you. Lean on Him. Put the full weight of your care and concern on Him. Allow Him to extend His mercies to you, to strengthen you so that you might endure and overcome, and to defeat evil on your behalf.

He *is* with you. Now and forever.

Make it your declaration today,

I have hope because God is
with me always!

CONCLUSION

HE GIVES US HOPE FOR TODAY

When we think of hope, we tend to think in terms of the distant future. Sometimes the present, however, seems so dark, so oppressing, so depressing, so suffocating that it is difficult even to anticipate living another day in such anguish.

I recently heard about a young man who is suffering greatly from a nerve-ending disorder. He lives in constant pain. This man said to a friend of mine, "When people talk about the future, I think of that as being about two hours from now."

His perspective is the one Jesus called us to have when He said, "Do not worry about tomorrow" (Matt. 6:34 NKJV). God always calls us to live in the *now*, to face the present honestly and fully, to do what we can do immediately, and to trust the future to God. Hope does not lie solely in anticipating that God will give us a wonderful future and resolve all things to our good. Rather, hope lies in knowing that God is with us in the here and now, and He will impart His love and grace to us to enable us to go from minute to minute, hour to hour, day to day.

God's love and grace are imparted to us in an ongoing flow— hourly, daily. God is the One who brings us not only through a period of struggle and sorrow, but also through each troublesome day.

Ask the Lord to kindle your hope that you might live faithfully for Him and in full reliance upon Him through *this* morning, then *this* afternoon, then *this* evening, and then *this* night.

God loves you, infinitely and unconditionally.

God has a master plan for all of creation, and you are a part of it. That plan is unfolding bit by bit, even today.

God has a blueprint for your life, which is also unfolding according to His timetable and His methods. A part of that purpose is unfolding today.

God still has more for you to be—He still is working in your life to transform you into the full likeness of Jesus Christ. Today is a day in which God is going to refine you yet a little more and bring you a little closer to His perfection for you.

God has more that He desires to communicate to you about Himself, about yourself, and about your purpose on the earth. He has something new to teach you today.

God has more for you to do in loving outreach to others. God has needs for you to meet in the lives of other people, needs that only you are fully qualified and capable of meeting. He will bring specific people with specific needs across your path today. He has a mission, or part of a mission, for you to accomplish between sunrise and sundown.

God believes in you and in the potential He built into you, and He is working in your life—even today—to bring you to a place of great meaning, purpose, and fulfillment.

God has promises of blessing that you haven't yet experienced, but that are on the way to you. Even now!

God is available to you and accepting of you every second of every day. He is your ever-present help, your "always and forever" Source of love and grace.

Take hope in who God is, specifically, who God desires to manifest Himself to be in your life *today*. He is your Hope. Anchor your soul in Him, and no storm can defeat you.

Yes, I have hope because God gives me His love and grace at the dawning of each new day. I am His and He is mine. He is my Hope!

About the Author

Charles Stanley is pastor of the 13,000-member First Baptist Church in Atlanta, Georgia. He is the speaker on the internationally popular radio and television program *In Touch*.

Twice elected president of the Southern Baptist Convention, Stanley received his bachelor of arts degree from the University of Richmond, his bachelor of divinity degree from Southwestern Theological Seminary, and his master's and doctor's degrees from Luther Rice Seminary.

Dr. Stanley is the author of many books, including *The Glorious Journey, The Source of My Strength, The Wonderful Spirit-Filled Life, The Gift of Forgiveness, How to Listen to God, Winning the War Within,* and *How to Handle Adversity*.